Raising Children
with Your
Heavenly Father

A Scripture-Based Parenting Guide

*May your walk mirror the dreams
you have for your children*

Susan Muns Parker

CLAY BRIDGES
P R E S S

Raising Children with Your Heavenly Father
A Scripture-Based Parenting Guide

Copyright © 2021 by Susan Muns Parker

Published by Clay Bridges in Houston, TX
www.claybridgespress.com

All rights reserved. No part of this publication may be reproduced, stored in a retrieval system, or transmitted in any form by any means, electronic, mechanical, photocopy, recording, or otherwise, without the prior permission of the publisher, except as provided for by USA copyright law.

Unless otherwise indicated, Scripture quotations are taken from the ESV® Bible (The Holy Bible, English Standard Version®), copyright © 2001 by Crossway, a publishing ministry of Good News Publishers. Used by permission. All rights reserved.

Scripture quotations marked (HCSB) are taken from the Holman Christian Standard Bible®, Copyright © 1999, 2000, 2002, 2003, 2009 by Holman Bible Publishers. Used by permission. HCSB® is a federally registered trademark of Holman Bible Publishers.

Scripture quotations marked (KJV) are taken from the King James Version (KJV): King James Version, public domain.

Scripture quotations marked (NIV) are taken from the Holy Bible, New International Version®, NIV®. Copyright ©1973, 1978, 1984, 2011 by Biblica, Inc.™ Used by permission of Zondervan. All rights reserved worldwide. www.zondervan.com The "NIV" and "New International Version" are trademarks registered in the United States Patent and Trademark Office by Biblica, Inc.™

Scripture quotations marked (NKJV) are taken from the New King James Version®. Copyright © 1982 by Thomas Nelson. Used by permission. All rights reserved.

Scripture quotations marked (TLB) are taken from The Living Bible copyright © 1971. Used by permission of Tyndale House Publishers, Inc., Carol Stream, Illinois 60188. All rights reserved.

Valentine illustration © 1972. Child Evangelism Fellowship Inc. All rights reserved. Adapted by permission.

ISBN: 978-1-953300-19-5
eISBN: 978-1-953300-20-1

Special Sales: Most Clay Bridges titles are available in special quantity discounts. Custom imprinting or excerpting can also be done to fit special needs. For standard bulk orders, go to www.claybridgesbulk.com. For specialty press or large orders, contact Clay Bridges at info@claybridgespress.com.

*Dedicated to
Our Heavenly Father*

My Prayer

Dear God in Heaven, gracious One,
Thank you for the things You've done.
When we are weak, You guide us through.
When we are strong, 'tis because of You.

When You are near to be our guide,
We know our fears will not abide.
With Your help, our lives are blessed
With joys supreme and eternal rest.

—Nancy Muns Leonard

Special Thanks

It is truly impossible to express my appreciation to Phil, my husband, for his unending help, encouragement, and support that enabled *Raising Children with Your Heavenly Father* to come to fruition.

Thank you, cousin Kathryn, for encouraging me to get serious and start writing this parenting guide before baby Rebekah was born. May not only your children, but may all children whose parents read this guide grow spiritually and develop a personal bond with their Heavenly Father.

Thanks to our daughter Pamela for always being available to brainstorm ideas, regardless of the time of day.

Thanks and appreciation to family and friends who have given me encouraging words, who have sought the Lord on my behalf, and who have proofed *Raising Children with Your Heavenly Father*. May the end result from all our labors of love result in a generation of children who walk with the Lord and who seek to please Him—a generation who is Heaven-bound.

I also appreciate Lucid Books for their expertise when it comes to publishing. Their various divisions beautifully handled each step necessary to prepare this book for publication.

I now challenge each person who reads this book to step up and nurture as many children as possible to walk with the Lord.

Table of Contents

Dedicated to Our Heavenly Father iii
Special Thanks v
The Importance of Planting Spiritual Seeds 1

Genesis 7
    Lesson 1: Allow Consequences to Follow Misbehavior 8
    Lesson 2: God Purged the Earth of Sin; Seek to Purge Your Family of Sin 10
    Lesson 3: Allow God to Orchestrate Your Children's Lives 12
    Lesson 4: Be a Role Model – Like Joseph 15

Exodus 19
    Lesson 1: Like Jochebed, Plant Spiritual Seeds 20
    Lesson 2: God Delivers the Ten Commandments to Moses 22
    Lesson 3: The Ten Commandments 25
    Lesson 4: A Study of the Ten Commandments 27
    Lesson 5: Do Not Follow the Crowd in Doing Wrong 34
    Lesson 6: Guardian Angels Are Available 36
    Lesson 7: Stop Generational Curses, and Create Generational Blessings 38

Leviticus 41
    Lesson 1: Teach Children to Obey God's Commandments 42
    Lesson 2: Rules for Living 44

Numbers 47
    Lesson 1: Make Restitution to Those You Wrong 48
    Lesson 2: Trust and Obedience Bring Success 50

Deuteronomy 53
    Lesson 1: Moses's Final Sermon 54
    Lesson 2: God Is Near When You Pray 56
    Lesson 3: Obedience Precedes Righteousness 58
    Lesson 4: National Wake-Up Call 59
    Lesson 5: Read God's Word for Spiritual Strength 61
    Lesson 6: America, Stay in Tune with God 63

Joshua 65
    Lesson 1: Total Obedience Brings Victory 66
    Lesson 2: Obedience Brings Success; Disobedience Brings Consequences 68
    Lesson 3: Mentor Your Replacement 70

Judges 73
    Lesson: God's Help Is Only a Prayer Away 74

Ruth 77
    Lesson: Naomi and Ruth: Exemplary Mother and Daughter-in-Law 78

1 Samuel 81
Lesson 1: God Hears a Mother's Prayer 82
Lesson 2: Dedicate Your Children to the Lord... 84
Lesson 3: You Reap What You Sow... 85
Lesson 4: Always Obey God.. 86
Lesson 5: Pray for Your Children and Others 88
Lesson 6: Successful as Judges; Failure as Parents 90
Lesson 7: Shun Evil, or Be Swept Away 92
Lesson 8: Inner Beauty Surpasses Outer Appearance 93
Lesson 9: The David and Goliath Story 95
Lesson 10: Choose to Return Evil with Kindness 97
Lesson 11: Abigail Reciprocated Kindness with Kindness 98

2 Samuel 101
Lesson 1: Fulfill All Your Pledges 102
Lesson 2: Confess and Seek Forgiveness for Your Sins 104
Lesson 3: Haughtiness Is a Sin 106

1 Kings 107
Lesson 1: David's Last Words to Solomon 108
Lesson 2: Solomon's Wisdom Awed Everyone 110
Lesson 3: Fervently Pray for Your Country as King Solomon Prayed for Israel 112

2 Kings 115
Lesson 1: Gehazi's Consequence for Lying: Leprosy 116
Lesson 2: Israel Responded with Kindness toward Their Enemy 118
Lesson 3: Successes and Failures Mirror Our Spiritual Walks 120

1 Chronicles 123
Lesson: Prepare Children for Success 124

2 Chronicles.. 127
Lesson 1: King Solomon: "Sinners: Pray, Repent, and Seek Forgiveness" 128
Lesson 2: King Abijah: "Rely on the Lord, Your God" 130
Lesson 3: King Asa: "Always Trust God!" 132
Lesson 4: King Joash: "Do Not Underestimate Generational Curses" ... 134
Lesson 5: King Uzziah: "Be Careful, Pride Goes before a Fall" 136
Lesson 6: King Josiah: "Read and Obey the Word of the Lord" 138

Ezra.. 141
Lesson: Prayers Move the Hand of God 142

Nehemiah 145
Lesson 1: Nehemiah Sought and Received God's Help 146
Lesson 2: To Experience Revival, Read His Word 148

Esther... 151
Lesson: Speak Up Boldly for the Lord 152

Job 155
Lesson 1: Listen with Your Heart-Be an Active Listener........................ 156
Lesson 2: Live Righteously, and Please Your Heavenly Father 157

Lesson 3: Do Not Judge Others—Comfort Them 158
Lesson 4: He Sees Our Every Step—Let Your Light Shine for Him 159
Lesson 5: Trust God in All Situations—He Is in Control 160
Lesson 6: Trust God Unconditionally 161

Psalms 163
Parenting Scriptures in Psalms 164

Proverbs and Ecclesiastes 173
Lesson 1: Wisdom Should Flow through Us to Our Children 174
Lesson 2: Flee Sexual Immorality 176
Lesson 3: Don't Be Lazy 178
Lesson 4: Seven Traits God Detests 180
Lesson 5: Transform Foolish Children into Wise Children 183
Lesson 6: Address Life's Issues with a Proverb 185

Isaiah 193
Lesson 1: Stop Doing Wrong; Learn to Do Right 194
Lesson 2: Refrain from Haughtiness 195
Lesson 3: Draw Near to Him 197
Lesson 4: Stand Firm in Your Faith Like King Ahaz 199
Lesson 5: Bond with Your Heavenly Father 201
Lesson 6: The Messiah Came as a Good Shepherd, with Power and Might 202
Lesson 7: God Gives Strength to the Weary 204
Lesson 8: Through Troubled Waters, God Is with Us 206
Lesson 9: God Can Blot Out Your Sins 208
Lesson 10: Receive Salvation and Eternal Life 209
Lesson 11: Our Beautiful World Reflects the Glory of God 211
Lesson 12: He Is the Potter; We Are the Clay 212

Jeremiah 215
Lesson 1: God Had a Plan for Jeremiah's Life, and He Has a Plan for Us 216
Lesson 2: America, Don't Ignore God 218
Lesson 3: Your Heart Determines Your Rewards 220
Lesson 4: May Each Generation Be Spiritually Strong 222

Lamentations 225
Lesson: During Difficult Times, Seek Your Heavenly Father 226

Ezekiel 229
Lesson 1: Plant God's Word in the Next Generation 230
Lesson 2: Who Is Responsible for Your Sins? 232

Daniel 233
Lesson 1: Take Care of Your Body 234
Lesson 2: Shadrach, Meshach, and Abednego Refused to Worship Idols 236
Lesson 3: Daniel Trusted God Even in a Lion's Den 238
Lesson 4: End Times: Separation of the Sheep and the Goats 241

Hosea 243
Lesson 1: Avoid Idolatry and Adultery 244
Lesson 2: Forgiveness Is Essential to Walk a Godly Path 245

Joel 247
    Lesson 1: The Locust Attack on Judah and Future Prophecy 248
    Lesson 2: Have a Heart for God's Family, Israel 250

Amos 253
    Lesson: Cities and Countries Reap What They Sow 254

Obadiah 257
    Lesson: Never Rejoice over Others' Misfortunes 258

Jonah 261
    Ten Lessons from the Book of Jonah 262

Micah 265
    Lesson: Children: Act Justly, Love Mercy and Walk Humbly with God 266

Nahum 269
    Lesson: God Disciplines the Ungodly 270

Habakkuk (Pre-Exilic Period) 273
    Lesson 1: The Just Shall Live by Faith, Regardless 274
    Lesson 2: Be Joyful through Troubled Times 275

Zephaniah (Pre-Exilic Period) 277
    Lesson: "Seek Ye the LORD while He May be Found" 278

Haggai (Post-Exilic Prophet) 281
    Lesson: Put God First 282

Zechariah (Post-Exilic Prophet) 285
    Lesson 1: Listen and Obey God's Word from the Pulpit 286
    Lesson 2: Why Are Your Prayers Not Answered? 288
    Lesson 3: Support Israel, God's Country 290

Malachi 291
    Lesson 1: Honor, Respect, Esteem, and Appreciate Your Heavenly Father and Your Earthly Parents 292
    Lesson 2: Be Equally Yoked 294
    Lesson 3: Prepare for the Second Coming of the Messiah (Jesus) 296
    Lesson 4: Parents, Teach Your Children to Tithe 298
    Lesson 5: God Wants Everyone to Know and Obey the Ten Commandments 301

Epilogue 302

References 303

The Importance of Planting Spiritual Seeds

A newborn baby is like freshly tilled soil just waiting to be seeded with spiritual seeds from above. God knows a baby's genetic makeup, and He knows the seeds that need to be planted in their lives to make them into the person He intended them to become. All children need a strong spiritual foundation to stay connected to their Heavenly Father throughout their lives. Parents also need spiritual nourishment to stay close to God while raising their children. As your children mature, remember to pray and seek wisdom from God, so they will remain on the road God intended for them to take and be prepared for heaven. You will enjoy peace as you watch your children walking in the ways of the Lord.

How do we build a strong spiritual foundation in the lives of our children? By planting spiritual seeds daily in their hearts. What a precious seed a mother plants when she sings "Jesus Loves Me" to her newborn. Additional seeds are planted every time someone reads a Bible story or sings a spiritual song to a child, or every time a child watches a spiritual video, attends a summer camp or vacation Bible school, or hears a prayer. What a special day it will be when your child prays and invites the Spirit of God to live in his or her heart! A person with the Holy Spirit within is grafted into the family of God and is Heaven-bound. Write the date that happens in your Bible—it is most special.

The secular world applauds earthly accomplishments; however, accolades will not open the doorway to Heaven. Satan smiles whenever we focus on earthly endeavors and leave the spiritual aspects of life on the back burner. Since our lifetimes are indeed very short compared to eternity, why do we plant so many here-and-now seeds instead of hereafter seeds? Because Satan works overtime to keep us focused on the here and now instead of the hereafter. He wants as many people as possible to awaken to eternal death, whereas our Heavenly Father desires that everyone awakens to eternal life in Heaven.

Spiritual seeds were planted in my heart at the age of seven while I was attending a vacation Bible school with a neighbor. Each day, we memorized Scripture and placed it in the fold of a fan. We also learned the song "There's within My Heart a Melody." At home, my friend and I skipped up and down the sidewalk singing our wonderful new song. It is still one of my favorites.

In my 30s, I learned of spiritual seeds that had been planted in my heart as a preschooler. It unfolded after buying a set of flannel-board Bible stories to teach preschoolers. When I showed them to my mother, she picked up the teacher's manual and exclaimed, "This author was our preacher in Pittsburgh; he taught a children's sermon every Sunday!" I have no memory of those sermons. Yet I probably received many spiritual seeds that strengthened my spiritual foundation and possibly gave me a heart for teaching children. I have now taught flannel-board Bible stories to preschoolers and school children for more than 30 years. They probably remember neither me nor the stories I taught, but I pray that the seeds planted in their hearts have developed and produced fruit in their lives.

May churches prioritize giving all children strong spiritual foundations. Children are like sponges—they readily absorb Bible stories, songs, and Scripture verses.

Bedtime is an incredible time to nurture children spiritually. Read them a Bible story, sing spiritual songs, pray the Lord's Prayer together, and pray for the needs of others.

During drive time, plant spiritual seeds in your children's hearts by playing CD Bible stories and singing spiritual songs. When shopping for others, consider choosing gifts that provide spiritual seeds.

There are many children who have not been blessed with spiritual foundations. When spiritually needy children cross your path, make a concerted effort to plant as many spiritual seeds as possible in their hearts, including the Ten Commandments. Invite them to attend church, Bible school, and a summer church camp. If possible, give them an age-appropriate Bible.

THE IMPORTANCE OF PLANTING SPIRITUAL SEEDS

We have nine months to prepare for our child's physical birth. Yet one's spiritual birthday (rebirth) can take an undeterminable number of years—maybe even a lifetime. We must never tire of preparing for it. Throughout children's lives, they receive many birthday presents from family and friends commemorating the day of their physical births. However, if all those gifts were gathered into one pile, they would be naught compared to the gift God gives them on their spiritual birthday. On that day, He gives them His Holy Spirit to indwell them this side of eternity, and at death, He enables them to join the family of God in Heaven.

We are babes in Christ after our spiritual rebirths, and changing from a newborn into a mature child of God takes time and effort. Satan cannot take away a person's salvation, but he can tarnish his or her Christian testimony. The more our children allow God to live in and through their lives, the more peace and joy we as parents experience and the brighter their lives shine for Him. Peace and joy are more satisfying than all the honors the world might bestow on them. May each of us as parents be able to proclaim, "I have no greater joy than to hear that my children are walking in the truth" (3 John 4).

If you have never had a time in your life when you invited the Holy Spirit to come into your heart, do not panic—it is *never* too late. Jesus led Nicodemus (an adult) to salvation one evening while they were talking. Nicodemus, a Jewish ruler, approached Jesus and asked Him what he could do to be saved. (Nicodemus recognized that Jesus had come from God because of His many miracles.) "Jesus answered him, 'Truly, truly, I say to you, unless one is born again he cannot see the kingdom of God'" (John 3:3).

Nicodemus then asked Jesus how a man could be born again since he cannot enter his mother's womb and be reborn.

> *Jesus answered, "Truly, truly, I say to you, unless one is born of **water** and the **Spirit**, he cannot enter the kingdom of God. That which is born of the flesh is flesh, and that which is born of the Spirit is spirit. Do not marvel that I said to you, 'You must be born again'"* (emphasis added).
> —John 3:5–7

Jesus wanted Nicodemus to understand that this rebirth referred to a *spiritual* birth, not a *physical* rebirth. "And as Moses lifted up the serpent in the wilderness, so must the Son of Man [Jesus] be lifted up, that whoever believes in him may have eternal life" (John 3:14–15). Jesus was referring to the cross when He spoke of the Son of Man being lifted up. He would die on the cross to take the punishment for our sins, making those who choose to spiritually embrace Him clean and prepared for Heaven.

Many have memorized these verses:

> *For God so loved the world that he gave his one and only Son, that whoever believes in him shall not perish but have eternal life. For God did not send his Son into the world to condemn the world, but to save the world through him. Whoever believes in him is not condemned, but whoever does not believe stands condemned already because they have not believed in the name of God's one and only Son. This is the verdict: Light has come into the world, but people loved darkness instead of light because their deeds were evil.*
>
> —John 3:16–19 NIV

Choosing to believe and receive the Light of the world is the most important decision parents and children make while on earth. Before Jesus returned to Heaven, He promised to send the Holy Spirit to live within us. The Holy Spirit is only a prayer away. Pray, and invite Him into your heart.

Before we jump in and start finding parenting Scriptures, know that we are not the first parents who needed help parenting. The first parents, Adam and Eve, had neither a Bible nor any self-help books to raise their children. They didn't even have the Ten Commandments. If Cain had learned not to covet or kill others, his jealous rage might have been contained and kept him from killing his brother, Abel.

When raising our children, I frequently quoted Scripture to guide them to walk a godly walk. If a problem arose in one of their lives, I would find Scripture to meet their need. (Today, the Internet is a great help. Just type a few words pertaining to your child's need, and usually several Scriptures will pop up.)

When parents correct minor misbehaviors, they probably protect their children from more serious wrongdoings. Teach your children that anything they do that does not please God is a sin. This book, *Raising Children with Your Heavenly Father*, is not a Bible study but a parenting guide that uses Scripture to raise godly children with integrity.

It is okay to earmark pages. This is a parenting guide. Highlight verses to use while teaching and training your children. You need not have Scripture perfectly memorized to use them—you can generalize their meanings, quote them to the best of your ability, or read them directly from the Bible. When you tell your children that God *expects* them to obey you, they listen. When a little boy became belligerent about putting his dirty paper plate in the trash, I looked at him and *calmly* said, "*God* wants you to obey me; (pause) put your plate in the trash." He quickly and quietly ran and threw his plate away. I was shocked. Even a little child knows to respect God.

May your family choose to "Seek the Lord while he may be found; call on him while he is near" (Isa. 55:6 NIV). Also, may your family's motto be, "As for me and my house, we will serve the Lord" (Josh. 24:15).

The Lord's Prayer
Matthew 6:9–13 KJV

Our Father which art in heaven, Hallowed be thy name.

Thy kingdom come, Thy will be done in earth, as it is in heaven.

Give us this day our daily bread.

And forgive us our debts, as we forgive our debtors.

And lead us not into temptation, but deliver us from evil: For thine is the kingdom, and the power, and the glory, for ever. Amen.

Genesis

In the first five books of the Old Testament, Moses records God's creation of the universe, the fall of humankind in the Garden of Eden, the Flood that destroyed the world, the reestablishment of humankind after the Flood, and the selection of Abraham and Sarah as the patriarch and matriarch of God's family, the Hebrew nation. In Genesis, we watch God move through the lives of the Hebrews. Here are three of the most dramatic days in the Hebrews' early history:

1. The day God parted the waters of the Red Sea, allowing several million Hebrews to cross on *dry* ground, freeing them from their Egyptian bondage
2. The day God gave Moses the Ten Commandments
3. The day the Hebrews entered the Promised Land after 430 years in Egypt and 40 years in the wilderness

Allow Consequences to Follow Misbehavior

Lesson 1: Genesis 4

After creating the universe and everything within it, God created the first man (Adam) and the first woman (Eve). They lived in the presence of God, and all was wonderful until, through the ploys of Satan, sin separated them from their Heavenly Father and tarnished their characters. Satan today still seeks to tarnish the character of every living man, woman, and child. God encourages godly behavior by allowing consequences to follow sins. Parents are God's agents to discipline and train children in the ways they should go.

Adam and Eve had two sons, Cain and Abel. Satan led Cain away from God and into sin.

> The LORD said to Cain, "Why are you angry, and why has your face fallen? If you do well, will you not be accepted? And if you do not do well, **sin is crouching at the door**. Its desire is contrary to you, but you must rule over it" (emphasis added).
>
> —Gen. 4:6–7

Cain became upset because God did not like his offering but was pleased with Abel's offering. Cain's covetousness intensified into a jealous rage, and he killed his brother. God then stepped forward and severely disciplined Cain: "When you work the ground, it shall no longer yield to you its strength. You shall be a fugitive and a wanderer on the earth" (Gen. 4:12). Because God had not yet given the Ten

Commandments to humankind, Cain had to learn the hard way to neither covet nor murder others.

When your children misbehave, it is easy to become angry and frustrated. Take time for the waters to calm, and then discuss their misbehavior. Ask them, "Which commandment did you break? God is displeased with your actions, but He does offer forgiveness." Explain that they need to go and sin no more. Like earthly parents, God, our Heavenly Father, desires to see His children obey Him because He knows what is best for them. If your child refuses to repent, *seek wisdom and discipline*. The purpose of discipline is to teach, train, and correct misbehavior, not just to punish.

Plant Spiritual Seeds

1. Learn from Cain's mistake. Do not covet, and do not murder. Satan is always planting sinful seeds and crouching at the door of our hearts to lead us astray.
2. "Your enemy the devil prowls around like a roaring lion looking for someone to devour" (1 Pet. 5:8 NIV).
3. Remind your children that sin is anything against God's commandments—it can even be a thought. Encourage your children to say no when tempted to sin.
4. Be sure your children know the Ten Commandments, and if they break a commandment, talk to them, and encourage them to go and sin no more.
5. Discipline should always follow repeated misbehaviors.

God Purged the Earth of Sin; Seek to Purge Your Family of Sin

Lesson 2: Genesis 6–9

Satan relentlessly attempts to draw people into sin. During the times of Noah, great wickedness and evil covered the entire earth, which made God grieve that He had ever created humankind. Therefore, He decided to wipe *all* people off the face of the earth.

Then He remembered that there was *one* righteous person—Noah.

God shared His plans with Noah. A flood would destroy all the people and animals on the face of the earth, but Noah's family, as well as seven pairs of every clean animal and one pair of every unclean animal, would find protection within an ark. Then God gave Noah detailed instructions for building an ark that could house his family and all the many animals, with plenty of food for those onboard.

Upon completion of the ark, Noah, his family, and all the animals entered it. *God* closed the door, and seven days later, all the springs from under the earth burst forth, and the floodgates of Heaven opened for the *first* time. Rain plummeted the earth for 40 days and nights, drowning all the people and animals outside the ark, while those inside the ark were safe and secure. After the floodwaters finally subsided, Noah, his family, and the animals left the ark to begin anew. God promised that He would never again flood the world, and to seal His covenant, He placed a rainbow in the sky.

Noah's family began to repopulate the earth. Through Noah's son Shem, a biblically significant family line arose—the family of

Abraham (Gen. 11:10, 27). He and his descendants would become what would one day be the nation of Israel (Matt. 1:1).

Plant Spiritual Seeds

1. There will *never* be another worldwide flood, but God will purge the earth again during the end times. At that time, God will separate the sheep (godly) from the goats (ungodly). The sheep will spend eternity in Heaven, while the goats will suffer eternal punishment (see Matt. 25:31–46).
2. When a rainbow appears in the sky, make it a teaching moment, and share the story of Noah and the ark. Remember, sin is very serious.

Allow God to Orchestrate Your Children's Lives

Lesson 3: Genesis 21–22, 24–25, 27, 29, 33

Abraham and Sarah were both well past childbearing ages when God selected them to become the patriarch and matriarch of His family. Abraham at age 100 and Sarah at age 90 were to have their first and only child, Isaac. When God asked Abraham to sacrifice Isaac in order to test Abraham's loyalty, Abraham promptly obeyed. After recognizing Abraham's willingness, God halted the sacrifice and gave Abraham a ram to sacrifice instead. Abraham had passed the test, and God proceeded with His plans to make Abraham's family *His* family. Ultimately, centuries later, Jesus would be born into the family of Abraham (Matt. 1:1). Many Old Testament prophecies pointed to Jesus's coming as well as His death, burial, and resurrection.

Abraham and Sarah's son, Isaac, married Rebekah. In time, she conceived twins, who fought continually within her womb. Concern filled Rebekah's heart, so she inquired of the Lord, who responded, "Two nations are in your womb, and two peoples from within you shall be divided; the one shall be stronger than the other, the *older* shall serve the *younger*" (emphasis added) (Gen. 25:23). Tradition dictated that the oldest child should receive the birthright and the father's blessing, but God had other plans. He told Rebekah that her *younger son*, Jacob, would rule over the *older son*, Esau.

In order for Jacob to become the patriarch of the family, he needed Esau's birthright and his father's blessing. Esau willingly gave Jacob his birthright for a bowl of soup. However, Jacob still needed to receive the blessing of his father Isaac before he passed.

One day, Rebekah overheard Isaac asking Esau to hunt for some wild game for them to eat because he wanted to give Esau his blessing before he died. After Esau left, Rebekah, knowing that Isaac's eyesight was greatly impaired, devised a plan so Jacob could receive the blessing instead of Esau. She called Jacob and asked him to get her two choice goats. She explained that she would prepare the meat, and then he could take it to his dad, eat with him (pretending to be Esau), and receive Esau's blessing. Rebekah also had Jacob put on Esau's best clothes and put goatskins on his arms and neck to better resemble his brother's hairy skin.

Jacob successfully deceived his dad and received the blessing due his brother. However, the deception angered Esau, and Jacob was forced to flee for his life.

Jacob supposedly went to his Uncle Laban's home in search of a wife, though in reality he lied to protect himself from his brother's wrath. While there, however, Jacob met Laban's beautiful daughter Rachel, who had an older sister named Leah. After Jacob had worked a month, his uncle offered to pay him for his labor. Jacob, however, asked if he could work seven years for the hand of Rachel. Laban agreed, and after seven years, Jacob prepared for his marriage to Rachel.

On the evening of the wedding, Laban deceived Jacob by swapping Rachel for Leah. Jacob did not realize the swap until the next morning, but when he complained, Laban said that it was only right that his older daughter marry first. He told Jacob to stay with Leah for a week, and then he could have the hand of Rachel—but he would need to work another seven years for Rachel.

Jacob and Rachel would have two sons, and he and Leah would have 10. Years later, Jacob took his family to Canaan. En route, he met Esau. When they saw each other, they wept and embraced. Jacob said, "For I have seen your face, which is like seeing the face of God, and you have accepted me" (Gen. 33:10). Esau had forgiven him.

Since God honored Jacob as Isaac's rightful heir, He changed Jacob's name to *Israel*, and his 12 sons and their families would become the 12 tribes of Israel. Esau's family would become the nation of Edom. His descendants, the Edomites, would forever resent Jacob and his family for taking Esau's birthright and blessing. The Edomites should have returned evil with kindness and overlooked the offense.

Plant Spiritual Seeds

1. The story of Jacob and Esau exemplifies this old adage: "Oh, what a tangled web we weave . . . when first we practice to deceive."[1] Rebekah set a poor example when she deceived Isaac into thinking Jacob was Esau. She should have remembered that nothing is too hard for God; He could have made Jacob the patriarch of His family without her help.
2. Each family member needs to discern God's plan for his or her life and fulfill it.

Be a Role Model – Like Joseph

Lesson 4: Genesis 37, 41–45

Joseph, one of Jacob (Israel) and Rachel's two sons, was a role model in righteous living. Joseph's story teaches children to be kind to those who are unkind to them. His story began when his 11 jealous brothers sold him into slavery and allowed their dad to believe that a ferocious animal had devoured him. Those who bought Joseph took him to Egypt and sold him to an officer of Pharaoh. As a slave, Joseph experienced much adversity, even imprisonment. But then the day came when Joseph interpreted Pharaoh's dream. "There will come seven years of great plenty throughout all the land of Egypt, but after them there will arise seven years of famine" (Gen. 41:29–30). Thereafter, Joseph's life completely changed. He left prison to live in a palace, and Pharaoh made him second in command over the entire nation.

As governor over Egypt, Joseph conceived a plan to combat the upcoming famine by storing grain during the seven years of plenty. When the drought finally arrived, it devastated not only Egypt but also the surrounding countries, including Canaan where Joseph's family lived. The famine became so devastating that Joseph's brothers had to travel to Egypt in search of food.

In a providential turn of events, Joseph recognized his brothers, had compassion on them, and gave them grain. He even returned the silver they had used to pay for the grain. Joseph set a godly example when he showed *kindness* and *mercy* instead of vindictiveness toward his unkind brothers. Later, he even invited his brothers to bring their families to Egypt because there were still five more years of famine. They did, and God, through Joseph, preserved the Hebrew nation.

This story is an excellent example of all things working together for good to those who love the Lord (Rom. 8:28). Joseph's trials and tribulations brought the Hebrews security and protection during the drought and after.

Plant Spiritual Seeds
1. Read the story of Joseph with your children, and teach them to be kind and merciful to those who are unkind to them.
2. Teach your children to be kind to their siblings.
3. Encourage your children to persevere through adversities because God works out *all* things for His glory and for their welfare (Rom. 8:28).

Exodus

Long after the seven-year drought, Joseph's brothers and their families remained in Egypt, growing stronger with each passing year. Their brief stay was extended to a total of 430 years. This additional time served a good purpose because God had foreordained that Abraham's family would multiply into a *great* nation. While in Egypt, the Hebrew nation prospered, and their descendants increased from 70 people to 600,000 men, plus women and children. Wow! The Hebrew people had become a great nation.

When a new pharaoh began ruling in Egypt, he became uncomfortable with the strength of the Hebrew people living within his country. Fearing that the Hebrews might rise up against Egypt, he forced them to become his slaves and commanded the midwives to kill all Hebrew baby boys. Because the midwives ignored Pharaoh's command, Pharaoh proclaimed a new decree that allowed all Egyptians to throw Hebrew baby boys into the Nile River.

However, nothing Pharaoh did could thwart God's plan for the Hebrews. God would intervene and protect a very special baby boy.

Like Jochebed, Plant Spiritual Seeds

Lesson 1: Exodus 2–3, 5, 14–15

Pharaoh's decree to eradicate all Hebrew baby boys had a glitch he did not anticipate. A precious mother, Jochebed, would devise a plan, *God's divine plan*, to save her son. *Under God's leadership*, she gently placed her baby into a waterproof basket and into the Nile River, probably praying that Pharaoh's daughter, the princess, would find him and protect him. The princess did find the baby floating among the reeds and immediately wanted to raise him as her own son.

When Miriam, the baby's sister, saw the princess's response, she offered to find a Hebrew woman to care for the baby until he was older. The princess agreed, and Miriam left, returning with Jochebed. What a blessing! Jochebed had the opportunity to train her *own* son in the ways of the Lord during his formative years and to teach him to love and pray to God Almighty. She planted *many spiritual seeds* in his heart. When the young boy was about six, Jochebed took him back to the palace, and the princess named him Moses. As the adopted grandson of Pharaoh, Moses received an excellent education and enjoyed a wonderful childhood.

One day, as an adult, Moses decided to wander into Hebrew territory because he was one of them. When he saw an Egyptian beating a Hebrew, anger surfaced, and he killed the Egyptian, which forced Moses to flee Egypt immediately. About 40 years later, God spoke to Moses in a burning bush and told him to go back to Egypt and set His people, the Hebrews, free. After questioning God, Moses finally agreed. He met up with his older brother, Aaron, and the two returned to Egypt.

Moses and Aaron approached Pharaoh and asked him to let the Hebrew nation leave Egypt. Pharaoh refused. However, after God allowed 10 plagues to attack the Egyptians, Pharaoh changed his mind and even provided supplies for the Hebrews' trip to the Promised Land.

But Pharaoh rescinded his willingness to let them leave. After all, he needed his slaves. He and his military pursued the Hebrews into the Red Sea. God provided a miraculous exit for His people by parting the waters of the Red Sea, allowing several million Hebrews to cross on *dry* ground. When the Egyptians followed them, the waters came crashing down, and all the Egyptians drowned.

Who orchestrated the fate of the Hebrew nation? God did.

Moses, with a heart for God, not only led the Hebrews out of bondage but also was the one to whom God entrusted the Ten Commandments.

Both Jochebed and Moses loved their Heavenly Father and served Him.

Plant Spiritual Seeds

1. Like Jochebed, plant many spiritual seeds in your children's hearts to give them a heart for God, a desire to pray regularly, and a longing to always seek His guidance.
2. Mothers, prepare your daughters for motherhood. All little girls need a doll to love and nurture. Rock your little daughter or granddaughter and together sing "Jesus Loves Me" to her baby doll.
3. Fathers, raise sons who will love and walk with the Lord.
4. Choose godly babysitters to care for your children.

God Delivers the Ten Commandments to Moses

Lesson 2: Exodus 19–20, 32

Three months after leaving Egypt, the Hebrews set up camp at the foot of Mount Sinai. God told Moses to meet Him on the mountain. Moses obeyed. There, Moses learned that if the Hebrews *obeyed God fully*, they would become *His treasured possession*. Moses returned to the camp and shared God's message. The Hebrews agreed to obey God fully. Moses then told them to wash their clothes and prepare to meet with God in three days.

> *On the morning of the third day there were thunders and lightnings and a thick cloud on the mountain and a very loud trumpet blast, so that all the people in the camp trembled. Then Moses brought the people out of the camp to meet God, and they took their stand at the foot of the mountain. Now Mount Sinai was wrapped in smoke because the L*ORD *had descended on it in fire. The smoke of it went up like the smoke of a kiln, and the whole mountain trembled greatly. And as the sound of the trumpet grew louder and louder, Moses spoke, and God answered him in thunder.*
>
> —Exod. 19:16–19

The Lord God called Moses to come back up the mountain and then asked him to go back down and warn the people to stay clear of the mountain and return with Aaron. After Moses and Aaron returned,

GOD DELIVERS THE TEN COMMANDMENTS TO MOSES

God spoke out the Ten Commandments, enabling *everyone* to hear them firsthand.

When Moses and Aaron descended Mount Sinai, they found a fearful nation, so Moses encouraged them, "Do not fear, for God has come to test you, that the fear of him may be before you, *that you may not sin*" (emphasis added) (Exod. 20:20). Moses then returned to the mountaintop *alone* and remained there *40 days and nights*. At the end of that time, God wrote the Ten Commandments on tablets of stone, and Moses returned to the camp carrying God's newly penned Ten Commandments.

But a shocking situation awaited Moses. Since Moses had been gone so long, the Hebrews had begun to fear that he would *never* return. Desiring something to worship, they sought Aaron's help to create an idol, and together they molded a golden calf from their melted jewelry. Upon its completion, the Hebrews began worshiping their human-made idol. At that time, Moses returned. Having just been in the presence of God Almighty and knowing that one of His commandments was to not worship idols, Moses became enraged and threw down the tablets, breaking them into many pieces.

This sinful nation needed discipline. Since punishment should follow sin, Moses took the golden calf they had made and melted it with fire. Then he ground it into powder, scattered it on the water, and made the Hebrews drink it. Yuck! Later, Moses returned to Mount Sinai where the Lord replicated the Ten Commandments on a new set of stones. The Hebrews had learned not to worship idols, and now they had nine more commandments to learn.

Plant Spiritual Seeds

1. Have a mindset to say no to idle worship.
2. Each generation needs to teach the next generation to pray *only to God Almighty* and not to idols. After asking our granddaughter Ella how she might teach a child not to worship idols, she came up with a clever idea using a hollow toy cow.

Idol Worship Is Worthless

Give your child a hollow toy cow, and do the following:
- Tap the cow. Does it sound hollow? (Yes)
- Tap your arm. Does it sound hollow?' (No)
- We are living people. We can hear, think, move, see, talk, and love. Can this hollow, toy cow hear, think, move, see, talk, and love? (No)
- Some people believe that an object like a human-made cow can answer prayers. Is that possible? (No)
- An object is not able to answer prayers. Even a golden cow cannot answer prayers. It is worthless to worship idols.

3. Only God can answer prayers. He created the world and made us in His image.
4. People have always had trouble keeping this commandment. Anything more important to you than God is your idol.

The Ten Commandments

Lesson 3: Exodus 20:1–17

Abraham Lincoln once said, "Without the Ten Commandments, we would not know right from wrong."[2] He remembered sitting on his mother's lap and learning the Ten Commandments.[3]

John Adams, the second president of the United States, said, "Without God and The Ten Commandments, it would be impossible to rule the world."[4]

The Ten Commandments, our moral laws, came directly from God Himself.

The Ten Commandments

I. "You shall *have no other gods before me*" (emphasis added) (Exod. 20:3).

II. "You shall *not make for yourself a carved image*, or any likeness of anything that is in heaven above, or that is in the earth beneath, or that is in the water under the earth. You shall not bow down to them or serve them, for I the LORD your God am a jealous God, visiting the iniquity of the fathers on the children to the third and the fourth generation of those who hate me, but showing steadfast love to thousands of those who love me and keep my commandments" (emphasis added) (Exod. 20:4–6).

III. "You shall not take the *name of the LORD your God in vain*, for the LORD will not hold him guiltless who takes his name in vain" (emphasis added) (Exod. 20:7).

IV. "*Remember the Sabbath day, to keep it holy*. Six days you shall labor, and do all your work, but the seventh day is a Sabbath to the Lord your God. On it you shall not do any work, you, or your son, or your daughter, your male servant, or your female servant, or your livestock, or the sojourner who is within your gates. For in six days the Lord made heaven and earth, the sea, and all that is in them, and rested on the seventh day. Therefore the Lord blessed the Sabbath day and made it holy" (emphasis added) (Exod. 20:8–11).

V. "*Honor your father and your mother*, that your days may be long in the land that the Lord your God is giving you" (emphasis added) (Exod. 20:12).

VI. "You shall *not murder*" (emphasis added) (Exod. 20:13).

VII. "You shall *not commit adultery*" (emphasis added) (Exod. 20:14).

VIII. "You shall *not steal*" (emphasis added) (Exod. 20:15).

IX. "You shall *not bear false witness* against your neighbor" (emphasis added) (Exod. 20:16).

X. "You shall *not covet* your neighbor's house; you shall not covet your neighbor's wife, or his male servant, or his female servant, or his ox, or his donkey, or anything that is your neighbor's" (emphasis added) (Exod. 20:17).

Plant Spiritual Seeds

1. Nancy Hanks Lincoln taught her son Abraham the Ten Commandments. Do likewise with your children.
2. Give each of your children an age-appropriate copy of the Ten Commandments, and explain each commandment in an age-appropriate manner.
3. Let your older children make their own copies of the Ten Commandments on quality paper and frame them. These handwritten copies will become wonderful keepsakes for the next generation.
4. Offer a monetary reward for memorizing the Ten Commandments—it has eternal value.
5. Blessings follow those who obey the Ten Commandments; refusing to obey God's commandments brings consequences.

A Study of the Ten Commandments

Lesson 4: Exodus 20:1–17

Commandment I

*You shall have **no other gods** before me* (emphasis added).
—Exod. 20:3 NIV

Our world was not a happenstance; instead, God Almighty, our Heavenly Father, foreordained it. His creation is truly marvelous in every way. Consider His sunsets, waterfalls, unique animals, birds, fish, and humans. He even has prepared a place for us in Heaven. Jesus announced this in the New Testament:

> *My Father's house has many rooms; if that were not so, would I have told you that I am going there to prepare a place for you? And if I go and prepare a place for you, I will come back and take you to be with me that you also may be where I am.*
> —John 14:2–3 NIV

Plant Spiritual Seeds

Worship only God Almighty, the Creator of the heavens and the earth, not idols.

Commandment II

You shall not make for yourself an image . . . for I, the Lord your God, am a jealous God, punishing the children for the sin of the parents to the third and fourth generation of those who hate me, but showing love to a thousand generations [our heirs] of those who love me and keep my commandments.
—Exod. 20:4–6 NIV

Our spiritual walk affects our heirs. If we love God and obey His commandments, our children are blessed, but if we ignore God, they may suffer consequences. I still remember seeing my paternal grandfather sitting in his chair reading his Bible. I believe his spiritual walk created generational blessings for our family.

Remember to always walk with the Lord and never worship or pray to idols.

Plant Spiritual Seeds

1. Never worship idols; only God can answer prayers.
2. In biblical days, people made objects to worship. Today, people tend to worship money, material possessions, celebrities, and so on. That is not good.
3. Both the Old and New Testaments teach that idol worship is a grave mistake.
4. To teach children that idol worship is worthless, return to page 24.

Commandment III

You shall not misuse the name of the L<small>ORD</small> your God, for the L<small>ORD</small> will not hold anyone guiltless who misuses his name.
—Exod. 20:7 NIV

Many emphasize a point or a concern by using a slang term for God or Jesus. Realize you are accountable to God if you abuse His or Jesus's name.

Plant Spiritual Seeds
1. Do not curse using the name of God or Jesus.
2. God's and Jesus's names are holy. If you are not directly talking about God or Jesus or praying to them, you are taking their names in vain. Revere God's and Jesus's names—do not abuse them.
3. Set an example for your children, and do not curse.

Commandment IV

Remember the Sabbath day by keeping it holy.
—Exod. 20:8 NIV

America has drifted away from this commandment. We find many people working and shopping on Sundays, which is not a healthy situation. Everyone needs to regroup, physically as well as spiritually. Sunday is that day.

Truett Cathy adhered to this commandment and brought honor to God by closing more than 1,950 Chick-fil-A restaurants on Sundays. Here's what the Chick-fil-A website says:

> Our founder, Truett Cathy, made the decision to close on Sundays in 1946 when he opened the first restaurant in Hapeville, Georgia. Having worked seven days a week in restaurants open 24 hours, Truett saw the importance of closing on Sundays so that he and his employees could set aside one day to rest and worship if they choose—a practice we uphold today.[5]

Cathy once said that closing on Sundays was one of the best business decisions he ever made. Interestingly, Chick-fil-A restaurants generate more sales in six days than most of their competitors generate in seven. Cathy gave the Lord credit for Chick-fil-A's success.

Oh, that Cathy might inspire those of you in the business world to follow his example and set your work aside on Sunday. Blessings will follow. It brought joy to my heart when I learned that Chip and Joanna Gaines, a godly entrepreneur couple in Waco, Texas, had also chosen to close their restaurant, Magnolia Table, as well as their retail stores on Sundays. What godly examples they set for the citizens of Waco, their state, and their country.

If your job requires you to work on Sundays, do not negate the importance of receiving spiritual food. Find a church that opens its doors on Friday or Saturday nights, and meet the spiritual needs of your family. Attending church honors God.

Plant Spiritual Seeds

1. Remember, God gave us the Sabbath and *commanded* us to keep it holy.
2. Make the Sabbath a day of rejuvenation, both spiritually and physically.
3. Create Sunday memories with your children.
4. Keep Sundays holy by taking care of your errands during the week.

Commandment V

> ***Honor*** *your father and your mother, so that you may live long in the land the* L<small>ORD</small> *your God is giving you* (emphasis added).
> —Exod. 20:12 NIV

God commands children to honor their parents and those to whom their parents have given charge. In a letter dated February 1952, Esther Ottison, a family friend, gave my parents this advice: "If your children are raised to respect their parents, it will always be wonderful for you."

Plant Spiritual Seeds

1. When children honor their parents, they please their Heavenly Father.
2. When children honor and obey their parents, they are blessed with a long life.
3. When children respond quickly to their parents' requests, they bring joy to their Heavenly Father.
4. Respectfully listen to your children.

Commandment VI

You shall not murder.
—Exod. 20:13 NIV

God values everyone's life. Children need to choose to be kind to others and please their Heavenly Father. God does not want us to hurt anyone physically, verbally, or emotionally.

Plant Spiritual Seeds

1. Teach children to value life.
2. Model kindness to your children, and expect them to treat others with kindness as well.

Commandment VII

You shall not commit adultery.
—Exod. 20:14 NIV

> ***Flee from sexual immorality.*** *Every other sin a person commits is outside the body, but the sexually immoral person sins against his own body. Or do you not know that your body is a temple of the Holy Spirit within you, whom you have from God? You are not your own, for you were bought with a price. So glorify God in your body* (emphasis added).
> —1 Cor. 6:18–20

Youths need to refrain from even a *hint* of sexual immorality. Protect your teenagers from opportunities to be tempted sexually. They need a mindset to say no *before* temptation occurs.

Those who are married need to be faithful to their spouse and, like youth, have a mindset to say no *before* temptation occurs.

Plant Spiritual Seeds

1. Flee from even a hint of sexual immorality. Do not allow your daughters to have a boy in your house unchaperoned or your sons to have a girl in your house unchaperoned.

2. Singles, reserve sex for marriage.
3. Teach your children to honor God with their bodies. Remember, the Holy Spirit lives within.

Commandment VIII

You shall not steal.
—Exod. 20:15 NIV

The New Testament adds, "Let the thief no longer steal, but rather let him labor, doing honest work with his own hands, so that he may have something to share with anyone in need" (Eph. 4:28).

If your children happen to steal and no one catches them, remind them that God sees them and that they are still accountable to Him. Be sure to discipline your children even if they steal only a piece of bubblegum.

Plant Spiritual Seeds

1. Do not steal. You are accountable to God.
2. Consequences should always follow stealing.
3. If your child steals, he or she must return the item and make restitution.
4. Teach a perspective of generosity in your home.

Commandment IX

You shall not give false testimony [lie] against your neighbor.
—Exod. 20:16 NIV

Never lie! God is the God of truth, and He wants us to be agents of truth as well.

Do not exaggerate the truth. There are no gray areas when it comes to telling the truth. If it is not the whole truth and nothing but the truth, it is a lie.

Plant Spiritual Seeds

1. Know that God is the God of truth. *Do not embellish* your stories.

2. Teach honesty to your children, and expect the truth. Lies are unacceptable.
3. Lying tarnishes one's testimony.

Commandment X

You shall not covet your neighbor's house. You shall not covet your neighbor's wife, or his male or female servant, his ox or donkey, or anything that belongs to your neighbor.
—Exod. 20:17 NIV

Contentment is a fleeting notion in today's society. Everyone should be content with what God has given them. Everything you have is from Him. Wanting what others have is telling God that He has not adequately provided for you.

Plant Spiritual Seeds
1. Be content with what God has given you, and do not covet what belongs to others.
2. Remember, Cain coveted his brother's righteousness and suffered serious consequences.
3. Jealousy and lusting for what others have is a sin.
4. If you have a need, seek God's help.

Throughout the Old Testament, people were encouraged to obey the Ten Commandments and teach them to their children. Remind your children that these are commandments, not options. Even though our public schools no longer teach the Ten Commandments, your children are still accountable to God to obey them.

Be responsible—teach your children the Ten Commandments.

Do Not Follow the Crowd in Doing Wrong

Lesson 5: Exodus 23

Do not follow the crowd in doing wrong.

—Exod. 23:2 NIV

This verse is applicable to everyone, regardless of age.

Before children can choose *not* to follow the crowd in doing wrong, they must know *right* from *wrong*. Parents who teach their children to live righteously will see their children living righteously. Children learn as they watch their parents and usually mimic their parents. If parents curse, children curse; if parents lie, children lie; if parents are honest, their children will probably be honest; if parents obey stop signs, their children will obey them. We all reap what we sow.

Be responsible, and raise your children to become godly citizens.

- Children need to know and obey not only the Ten Commandments and the many other biblical lessons found throughout the Bible but also the laws of our city, state, and national governments.
- Live out the Golden Rule: "Do to others as you would have them do to you" (Luke 6:31 NIV).
- Read books and watch videos with your children that teach integrity (for example, *Uncle Arthur's Bedtime Stories*, *VeggieTales*, and *Superbook*).

- Do not drive while under the influence of drugs or alcohol or while using your cell phone.
- Always obey speed limits, and use your turn signals.
- Do not litter; take care of God's beautiful world.
- Say no to drugs and alcohol.
- Make sure your children obey your rules at home.

Plant Spiritual Seeds

1. Memorize Exodus 23:2 NIV: "Do not follow the crowd in doing wrong."
2. Your children need to know every law and rule that you expect them to obey.
3. By using role-play, teach your children to make wise choices. Give them a predetermined mindset to do what is right, even when a friend chooses to do wrong. For example, ask your child, "What would you do if someone offered you drugs?" Then add, "Let's not hurt ourselves; you know drugs are additive." Everyone needs to say no, not only to drugs but also to lying, stealing, immorality, coveting, hurting others, drinking, and more.
4. Memorize Psalm 119:11: "I have stored up your word in my heart, that I might not sin against you."

Guardian Angels Are Available

Lesson 6: Exodus 23

Angels are real heavenly beings created by God, and they are available to protect us. Exodus 23:20 explains, "Behold, I send an angel before you to guard you on the way and to bring you to the place that I have prepared." In the Psalms we read, "For he will command his angels concerning you to guard you in all your ways. On their hands they will bear you up, lest you strike your foot against a stone" (Ps. 91:11–12).

I asked a family friend, Johnny Murphy, if he had ever experienced angelic protection. He responded yes, while he was in high school. Here's his story.

When Johnny and a friend were driving to a hot-rod meeting, a train that was backing up on the track hit them and pushed them down the track about 100 yards, gradually crushing their car. After it stopped, they walked away uninjured. Later, the boys learned that the conductor had failed to turn on the intersection's warning lights. When Johnny took his mom to see the crushed car, she fainted. It was obvious that these two boys had had angelic protection.

A neighbor, Gloria Humphreys, had an equally amazing angelic experience. In an earlier marriage, she was extremely poor. Her husband had filled her car with gas, or so he said, and she and her friend left to enjoy an evening of fellowship. As they were getting onto the bypass, her car stopped; it was out of gas. They sat there, not knowing what to do, and then a man stopped behind them who had an unbelievably kind countenance. He asked if he could help. After they explained that they were out of gas, he offered to take my friend to a gas station if she would return the gas can to the station. Feeling completely comfortable, she accepted his offer, and they left for the gas station. Upon their return, he put the gas into her tank. She hopped into her car and turned around to say thank you, but mysteriously, he was gone, as was his car. She and her friend knew immediately that he was not just an ordinary man, but an angel. When she returned the gas can, the attendant said the gentleman had left a $20 bill to fill up her car with gas. They were awed.

These stories are beautiful testimonies that God can protect and provide for those in need.

Plant Spiritual Seeds

1. Remind your children that God can provide angelic protection.
2. Pray a hedge of protection around each of your children (see Job 1:10).
3. Give your heart a good examination. Are you seeking to please the Lord or people? Ask friends if they have experienced angelic protection. You might hear some amazing stories. Have your friends share their stories with your children.

Stop Generational Curses, and Create Generational Blessings

Lesson 7: Exodus 34

We should be careful how we live because God "punishes the children and their children for the sin of the parents to the third and fourth generation" (Exod. 34:7 NIV). Think back three generations, or read old letters, and try to determine your family's generational weaknesses or sinful patterns. Once you are aware of them, talk with your children, and share ways to break the chain of sin. Children need to have a mindset to say no when faced with a generational curse or a sinful pattern. However, make sure you clarify that just because an ancestor was an alcoholic does not mean that the third and fourth generations will become alcoholics. It only means they could be tempted by alcohol.

If there are generational curses (weaknesses), there must also be generational blessings. If parents are loving and kind, their children will probably be loving and kind. That would indeed be a blessing. When we sow godly seeds, our children exhibit godly behavior.

Parents, make a concerted effort to set godly examples for your children. Parents have no control over previous generational curses, but they can be instrumental in breaking loose from curses and creating blessings. It might take several generations to succeed. What kind of legacy do you want to pass down to the next generation? Choose a godly one.

Plant Spiritual Seeds

1. Determine your family's generational weaknesses or sinful patterns, and teach your children to have a mindset to say no when tempted with these issues.
2. Do not add new generational curses to your family's legacy; instead, plant generational blessings and positive patterns.

Leviticus

Moses and Aaron were brothers from the tribe of Levi (Jacob and Leah's third son). Moses went down in history because he led the Hebrew nation out of Egypt and because God chose him to be the recipient of the Ten Commandments. Aaron and his descendants, the priestly tribe, were responsible to lead the Hebrew nation spiritually, embedding the Ten Commandments in their hearts.

In Leviticus, Moses reiterates the importance of keeping the Ten Commandments as well as the many additional rules for living a God-pleasing life.

God had plans for Moses and Aaron, and He has plans for each of us. Step up, pray, and fulfill His plans for your life.

Teach Children to Obey God's Commandments

Lesson 1: Leviticus 10

Aaron learned the value of parental discipline the hard way. Two of his four sons died because he had not taught them to obey God explicitly. In Leviticus, a generational curse was placed on Aaron's family:

> Now Nadab and Abihu, the sons of Aaron, each took his censer and put fire in it and laid incense on it and offered **unauthorized fire** before the Lord, which he had **not** commanded them. And fire came out from before the Lord and consumed them, and they **died** before the Lord (emphasis added).
>
> —Lev. 10:1–2

God got Aaron's attention.

Later, Moses spoke to Aaron and his two remaining sons, Eleazar and Ithamar. "Take the grain offering that is left of the Lord's food offerings, and eat it unleavened beside the altar, for it is most holy" (Lev. 10:12). Did Aaron and his two sons obey Moses's command? Yes, they most definitely did. They had learned firsthand that consequences follow disobedience. God does not want lukewarm Christians. Obedience is never an option—it is mandatory.

If Aaron had effectively taught *all* his boys to obey God, Nadab and Abihu would not have offered *unauthorized* fire before the Lord.

The same is true in families today. We need to teach our children God's commandments; if they miss the mark, there should be consequences.

Continually train and guide your children in the ways of the Lord.

Plant Spiritual Seeds

1. Teach your children to obey all God's commandments, especially the Ten Commandments.
2. Discipline is not punishment; it is *teaching* your children to obey God.
3. Consequences usually correct disobedience. Sometimes, there are natural consequences that are sufficient; other times, parents need to institute a consequence.
4. Grandparents, pray that your children will effectively discipline your grandchildren.

Rules for Living

Lesson 2: Leviticus 19

Leviticus 19 contains additional rules for living.

1. "The wages of a hired worker shall not remain with you all night until the morning" (Lev. 19:13).
   - Pay wages promptly.
2. "You shall not curse the deaf or put a stumbling block before the blind, but you shall fear your God: I am the Lord" (Lev. 19:14).
   - Be kind to the disabled.
3. "You shall do no injustice in court. You shall not be partial to the poor or defer to the great, but in righteousness shall you judge your neighbor" (Lev. 19:15).
   - Do what is right and fair in the courtroom.
4. "You shall not go around as a slanderer among your people" (Lev. 19:16).
   - Say only what is kind; do not gossip or speak ill of others.
5. "You shall not take vengeance or bear a grudge against the sons of your own people, but you shall love your neighbor *as yourself*: I am the Lord" (emphasis added) (Lev. 19:18).
   - Forgive and love others as you love yourself.
6. "You shall not eat any flesh with the blood in it. You shall not interpret omens or tell fortunes" (Lev. 19:26).
   - Do not practice divination or sorcery or delve into witchcraft.

7. "You shall keep my Sabbaths and reverence my sanctuary: I am the Lord" (Lev. 19:30).
   - At church, we should focus on Him, not ourselves. We attend church to honor God and to worship Him. Train your children to be reverent in church.
8. "You shall stand up before the gray head and honor the face of an old man, and you shall fear your God: I am the Lord" (Lev. 19:32).
   - Stand up and say hello to older people when they come into a room. Treat the elderly with honor and respect.
9. "You shall do no wrong in judgment, in measures of length or weight or quantity" (Lev. 19:35).
   - Be an honest person with integrity.

When we live according to His Word, we please our Heavenly Father.

Plant Spiritual Seeds
1. Children have many rules to learn. Instead of presenting rules in a negative way for everything we should not do, explain that rules are for *our own good* so we can enjoy a blessed life.
2. As a family, focus weekly on one of the verses from Leviticus 19.

Numbers

The most valuable lesson parents learn in the book of Numbers is that an *unrepentant,* disobedience person will face consequences. The adults who left Egypt, with the exception of Joshua and Caleb, never entered the Promised Land because they did not trust God enough to obey Him. They failed to remember that when God tells His people to do something, He prepares them for success.

Make Restitution to Those You Wrong

Lesson 1: Numbers 5

> The LORD said to Moses, "Say to the Israelites: 'Any man or woman who wrongs another in any *way and so is unfaithful to the* LORD *is guilty and must confess the sin they have committed. They must make full restitution for the wrong they have done, add a fifth of the value to it and give it all to the person they have wronged.'"*
>
> —Num. 5:5–7 NIV

When our granddaughter was three, I read her a story from *Uncle Arthur's Bedtime Stories* about a little girl who had to make restitution because she had cut her friend's dress. Her parents made her give that friend her *new* dress. Our granddaughter liked saying the word *restitution* and learned its meaning because of the story. She kept telling me, "I am not going to cut the dress, SuSu [her nickname for me]." Reading to your children not only encourages literacy and vocabulary but can also teach moral lessons. Through this story, she learned the importance of showing kindness toward others. If we fail to teach children godly behaviors, it most likely will become necessary to correct misbehaviors.

One of my friends has an adopted granddaughter from Ukraine. This granddaughter learned about making restitution the hard way.

In Ukraine, she had never learned the Ten Commandments. She did not know stealing was unacceptable. After starting school in America, she took a friend's bonus bucks because she wanted more bucks. At that point, her parents knew they needed to teach her the eighth commandment, "You shall not steal" (Exod. 20:15), and the 10th commandment, "You shall not covet" (Exod. 20:17). Her parents made her give that friend her favorite stuffed animal to teach her not to covet or steal.

Plant Spiritual Seeds

1. Learning not to steal is a valuable lesson.
2. Making restitution to others is an effective way to teach children not to steal or covet. Children should also apologize for their wrongdoings and seek *God's forgiveness.*
3. As a child, I enjoyed *Uncle Arthur's Bedtime Stories*, as did our children and now our grandchildren. Google *Uncle Arthur's Bedtime Stories*, and share these stories with your children. Purchase videos, Bibles, devotionals, storybooks, and secular books that teach children moral lessons. It will be money well spent.
4. Give your child a mindset to never repeat a wrongdoing. Teach them to go and sin no more. God forgives a repentant heart.
5. Wisely determine how to correct your child's misbehavior. A serious talk is frequently all it takes. Regardless, seek God's guidance if you administer discipline.
6. After disciplining your child, reaffirm your love and God's love for them.

Trust and Obedience Bring Success

Lesson 2: Numbers 13–14

When God gives you a task to do, trust and obey Him, and you will enjoy success.

When the Hebrew people were ready to enter the Promised Land, God told Moses to select a leader from each of the 12 tribes to explore and spy out the land. After exploring the land for 40 days, they returned and reported that the land did flow with milk and honey. As evidence, they presented a cluster of grapes so large that it took two men to carry it. They also reported that the people were powerful and their cities strongly fortified. At this, fear penetrated the camp.

Then Caleb, a spy who trusted God, spoke out, "Let us go up at once and occupy it, for we are well able to overcome it" (Num. 13:30). Joshua agreed with Caleb, but the remaining 10 spies described the people as strong giants. "We seemed like grasshoppers in our own eyes, and we looked the same to them" (Num. 13:33 NIV).

The Hebrew nation sided with the 10 fearful spies. They bemoaned the fact that they had ever left Egypt. "And they said to one another, 'Let us choose a leader and go back to Egypt'" (Num. 14:4).

Moses and Aaron were distraught, as were Joshua and Caleb, who reminded the Hebrew assembly:

> The land, which we passed through to spy it out, is an exceedingly good land. If the LORD delights in us, he will bring us into this land and give it to us, a land that flows with milk and honey. Only do not rebel against the LORD. And do not fear the people of the land, for they are bread for

us. Their protection is removed from them, and the Lord *is with us; do not fear them.*

—Num. 14:7–9

Joshua and Caleb's confidence in God angered the Hebrews to the extent that they wanted to stone the two men. But suddenly, the glory of the Lord appeared at the tabernacle and spoke to Moses:

How long will this people despise me? And how long will they not believe in me, in spite of all the signs that I have done among them? I will strike them with the pestilence and disinherit them, and I will make of you a nation greater and mightier than they.

—Num. 14:11–12

Moses pleaded with God to forgive the sins of His people.

Then the Lord *said, "I have pardoned, according to your word. But truly, as I live, and as all the earth shall be filled with the glory of the* Lord, **none** *of the men who have seen my glory and my signs that I did in Egypt and in the wilderness, and yet have put me to the test these ten times and have not obeyed my voice, shall see the land that I swore to give to their fathers. And none of those who despised me shall see it"* (emphasis added).

—Num. 14:20–23

God kept His promise in Numbers 14:18:

The Lord *is slow to anger and abounding in steadfast love, forgiving iniquity and transgression, but he will by no means clear the guilty,* **visiting the iniquity of the fathers on the children, to the third and fourth generation** (emphasis added).

The adults who did not trust God would never enter the Promised Land. Since Joshua and Caleb trusted God, they qualified to enter. Even though the adults had learned their lesson the hard way, they had 40 years to teach the next generation to trust and obey God and listen and follow the new prophet (preacher), Joshua. Through spiritual nurturing, these desert children did learn *to trust and obey God at all times*; our children need to learn this same lesson. Parents, teachers, and preachers, embrace the importance of shaping and molding godly behavior and the moral compasses of *all* children. They are the foundation that will keep a nation spiritually strong.

Plant Spiritual Seeds
1. Learn from the Hebrews' mistake. *Trust* and *obey* God, and avoid wandering in your own desert unnecessarily for an undetermined time.
2. Be positive, and remember that God is in control of the world. Seek His guidance in your life.
3. Sin is serious; we are all accountable for our walks. Remember, God will visit "the iniquity of the fathers on the children, to the *third and fourth generation*" (emphasis added) (Num. 14:18).

Deuteronomy

At the end of his life, Moses wrote the book of Deuteronomy to give the Hebrew people directives as they prepared to enter the Promised Land. He knew that he would not be going into the land and that the Hebrew children must obey God explicitly in order to succeed. Their degree of success would be determined by their degree of obedience. Moses continually emphasized the importance of obedience, and thus there is much repetitiveness in Deuteronomy.

Even today, obedience to God keeps a nation strong. Moses's last sermon to the Hebrews is a relevant sermon for any parent, any group, or any nation today.

Moses's Final Sermon

Lesson 1: Deuteronomy 4, 6

Moses took advantage of his final moments with the Hebrew nation to give them encouraging words before they entered the Promised Land. Indeed, Joshua, Caleb, and the younger generation of Hebrews were ready to trust and obey God as they prepared to claim the Promised Land. Moses's heartfelt words were vital for the Hebrews' future success and are relevant for us today.

> *Only take care, and keep your soul diligently, lest you forget the things that your eyes have seen, and lest they depart from your heart all the days of your life.* **Make them known to your children and your children's children.** *. . . And he [the Lord] declared to you his covenant, which he commanded you to perform, that is, the Ten Commandments, and he wrote them on two tablets of stone. And the* LORD *commanded me at that time to teach you statutes and rules, that you might do them in the land that you are going over to possess. . . .* **You shall love the** LORD **your God with all your heart and with all your soul and with all your might.** *And these words that I command you today shall be on your heart. You shall teach them* **diligently** *to your children, and shall talk of them when you* sit *in your house, and when you* **walk** *by the way, and when you* lie **down**, *and when you rise. You shall bind them as a sign on your hand, and they shall be as frontlets [ornaments] between your eyes. You shall write them on the doorposts of your house and on your gates* (emphasis added).
>
> —Deut. 4:9, 13–14; 6:5–9

Do not neglect the Bible as you raise your children. Talk with your children about God until you embed His teachings in their hearts and minds. May our children live godly lives and bring glory to God.

Plant Spiritual Seeds

1. Encourage children to keep the Ten Commandments and "love the LORD your God with all your heart and with all your soul and with all your strength" (Deut. 6:5 NIV).
2. Moses encouraged parents to teach their children the ways of the Lord every day while sitting, walking, talking, and thinking, and to remember to draw near to Him at bedtime as well as in the morning.
3. May many spiritual seeds germinate and grow in your children's hearts.
4. Ultimate joy is seeing grandchildren walking in the footsteps of Jesus. May generational blessing flow through your family.

God Is Near When You Pray

Lesson 2: Deuteronomy 4

Help your children realize that their prayers are not mere words. Remind them that they are literally talking to their Heavenly Father, the Creator of the heavens and the earth. Deuteronomy 4:7 says, "For what great nation is there that has a god so near to it as the LORD our God is to us, whenever we call upon him?"

To understand the presence of God, have your children place their palms facing each other. Let one palm symbolize God sitting on His throne in Heaven, listening and talking to you, and the other palm symbolize your listening and talking to your Heavenly Father. Then look up toward Heaven, close your eyes, and visualize Him seated on His throne. Sense His presence as you talk to Him. Then be still, and listen for a word or a thought from Him. Conclude your prayer with this: "May your will be done in my life. In Jesus's name I pray, Amen." Jesus intercedes for us to our Heavenly Father.

At bedtime, pray the Lord's Prayer (Matt. 6:9–15) with your children, and add this: "For Thine is the kingdom and the power and the glory forever, Amen." *Omit words* from the prayer, and let your children fill in the correct words. In time, they will have memorized the Lord's Prayer.

Plant Spiritual Seeds

1. Remind your children that God hears their prayers.
2. Pray with your children before meals, before they leave for school, at bedtime, and any time they have a problem.

3. Pray for your children throughout each school day.
4. Encourage your children to seek the Lord's help as they do their homework and prepare for tests. Remind them to even seek His help during tests. (Once, I sought the Lord's help while taking a test; He jarred my memory bank, and I remembered the answer.)

Obedience Precedes Righteousness

Lesson 3: Deuteronomy 6

And it will be righteousness for us, if we are careful to do all this commandment before the LORD our God, as he has commanded us.

—Deut. 6:25

When we *obey God*, we become righteous in His eyes. *Righteousness* means right standing before God. Though we will never be perfect and are all tarnished, when we seek to obey Him, we are approaching righteousness.

Plant Spiritual Seeds

1. Frequently remind your children that *obedience precedes righteousness*.
2. May the Holy Spirit nudge us to hear and obey our Heavenly Father.
3. Pleasing God should bring personal satisfaction in and of itself. Draw a parallel between times when your children were obedient and a possible blessing that followed.
4. Memorize James 5:16 NIV: "The prayer of a righteous person is powerful and effective."

National Wake-Up Call

Lesson 4: Deuteronomy 8

What does it take to keep a nation strong? Do not forget God! Moses emphasized this point to the Hebrews:

> *Take care lest you forget the L*ORD *your God by not keeping his commandments and his rules and his statutes, which I command you today, lest, when you have eaten and are full and have built good houses and live in them, and when your herds and flocks multiply and your silver and gold is multiplied and all that you have is multiplied, then your heart be lifted up, and you **forget** the L*ORD *your God, who brought you out of the land of Egypt, out of the house of slavery* (emphasis added).
>
> —Deut. 8:11–14

God warned the Hebrews that if they forgot Him and began to worship idols, they would face destruction. Sounds like a wake-up call for America! Like Israel, godly principles laid the foundation for America, yet today, many in America block efforts to teach children the Ten Commandments. Have Americans had so much of the good life that they do not need God? Has America forgotten God?

Teach your children God's Word. Don't merely rely on the church to teach them. Children need more than the hour they receive on Sundays.

When our granddaughter came for a visit, we went to the mall. When we came to a double-sided copy of the Ten Commandments, we sat down, and I read the Ten Commandments to her. What a wonderful opportunity the mall provided us! Perhaps the morality of our country would improve if more copies of the Ten Commandments were accessible to the public.

Plant Spiritual Seeds

1. Know the Bible so you can teach the Bible to your children and grandchildren.
2. *Pray* with your children that America returns to her strong, Christian heritage.
3. Home-school your children in the Word of God.
4. Strive daily to grow spiritually by reading the Bible or a devotional book, praying, listening to music, and serving others.
5. On Sundays, attend church.

Read God's Word for Spiritual Strength

Lesson 5: Deuteronomy 31

Every seven years, God commanded the priest to do this:

> *Assemble the people, men, women, and little ones, and the sojourner within your towns, that they may **hear and learn** to fear the LORD your God, and **be careful to do all the words of this law**, and that their children, who have not known it, may hear and learn to fear the LORD your God, as long as you live in the land that you are going over the Jordan to possess* (emphasis added).
>
> —Deut. 31:12–13

In biblical days, the Scriptures were not readily available, so whenever a priest read the Word, people listened. Imagine if you only *heard* the Word every seven years how special that reading would be. We have many opportunities to hear and read the Word, but how intently do we really listen, and how seriously do we follow its teachings?

Parents reinforce the Word when they live out the Word in their lives. Make every effort to teach God's Word to your children and grandchildren.

Plant Spiritual Seeds

1. Give your children an age-appropriate Bible or devotional book to read. Cuddle with your younger ones, and read the Word together.

2. Encourage your children to be good listeners and live out the sermons and Bible lessons they hear. As you read to your children, ask questions to verify that they heard the Word.
3. Each generation is responsible to pass the Word down to the next generation.

America, Stay in Tune with God

Lesson 6: Deuteronomy 31

God told Moses that the people would eventually fall away from Him.

> *This people will rise and whore* [prostitute] *after the foreign gods among them in the land that they are entering, and they will forsake me and break my covenant that I have made with them.*
>
> —Deut. 31:16

How did God know that they would fall away from Him? Because He knew their hearts.

God declared that He would hide His face from them and many disasters and difficulties would befall them. Years later, God's Word came true. The Israelites were deported to Assyria indefinitely because they walked away from their Heavenly Father, and 100 years later, the Judeans would forsake the Lord and be deported to Babylonia for 70 years. Why did these countries face deportation? They *ignored God* and *worshiped idols*.

Remember, disobedience calls for discipline.

Like Israel and Judah, America is forsaking the Lord and her spiritual heritage. America is on a slippery slope that could lead to her demise. Does God have reasons to be angry with America? Yes, He does.

Let us not disappoint God but finish strong by repenting and returning to the God of our fathers. Strengthen America one family at a time.

Plant Spiritual Seeds
1. You may not realize what you have sown into your children's lives, but future generations certainly will. Seek long-term benefits. May your grandchildren and great-grandchildren walk with the Lord and serve Him.
2. Have endurance and perseverance to finish strong. Life, as well as parenting, is a marathon, not a sprint. Stay faithful.
3. Together make plans to strengthen your family spiritually.

Joshua

After the Hebrew people accepted Joseph's invitation to move to Egypt and spent 430 years there, they experienced a miraculous exit out of Egypt only to face a 40-year stint in the desert for disciplinary reasons. Finally, the day arrived and they eagerly prepared to take the land promised to Abraham.

God chose Joshua, whom Moses had mentored, to lead the Hebrews into the Promised Land. Battles ensued, and Joshua learned immediately that if his army explicitly *obeyed God*, they would *be successful* on the battlefield. In time, the Promised Land was in the hands of the Hebrews (Israelites) and divided among 11 of its 12 tribes. Aaron's priestly tribe, the Levities, did not receive a portion of land because they served the Lord throughout all Israel. However, they did receive pastureland for their animals.

Total Obedience Brings Victory

Lesson 1: Joshua 6

The book of Joshua is exciting. Joshua's conquest of the Promised Land began with a miracle. As the priests stepped into the Jordan River to cross into Jericho, the waters parted, and the Israelites crossed over on *dry ground*. This reminded the people of their ancestors who had crossed the Red Sea on *dry ground* as they escaped Egypt. This miracle was confirmation that God was now with Joshua, as He had been with Moses.

Their first battle, the Battle of Jericho, was quite interesting. God orchestrated it as follows:

> *You shall march around the city, all the men of war going around the city once. Thus shall you do for six days. Seven priests shall bear seven trumpets of rams' horns before the ark. On the seventh day, you shall march around the city seven times, and the priests shall blow the trumpets. And when they make a long blast with the ram's horn, when you hear the sound of the trumpet, then all the people shall shout with a great shout, and the wall of the city will fall down flat, and the people shall go up, everyone straight before him.*
>
> —Josh. 6:3–5

The battle was unique and successful because they explicitly followed God's plans.

Plant Spiritual Seeds
1. Obedience precedes success.
2. Seek God's plans before you start a new day or a new project, or make an important decision.

Obedience Brings Success; Disobedience Brings Consequences

Lesson 2: Joshua 7

The battle of Jericho came off without a hitch—or did it? Little did Joshua know that one of his men had secretly stolen gold, silver, and a beautiful robe during the battle. *Stealing* was (and is) a sin against God; thus, they were doomed for failure when they faced the next city, Ai. The battle was a disaster, and the Lord explained why.

> *Israel has sinned; they have transgressed my covenant that I commanded them; they have taken some of the devoted things; they have* **stolen** *and* **lied** *and put them among their own belongings. Therefore the people of Israel cannot stand before their enemies. They turn their backs before their enemies, because they have become devoted for destruction. I will be with you no more, unless you destroy the devoted things from among you* (emphasis added).
>
> —Josh. 7:11–12

Joshua gathered the 12 tribes of Israel together and demanded the stolen items be returned to the Lord's treasury. Then God revealed to Joshua the guilty tribe, the guilty clan, the guilty household, and finally, the guilty family. Achan and his family stepped forward, and Achan confessed that he was the one who had sinned. He explained that when he saw the beautiful robe from Babylon and the silver and gold, he *coveted* them, *took* them, and *hid* them in the ground under his tent.

Achan, his family, and all his animals and belongings were taken to Joshua in the Valley of Achor. "Joshua said, 'Why have you brought this trouble on us? The Lord will bring trouble on you today'" (Josh. 7:25 NIV). That day, Achan did reap what he had sown; he was stoned, along with his family and animals. His possessions were burned.

The Israelites learned that it would take explicit obedience to successfully take possession of the land promised to Abraham. Obedience brings success.

Plant Spiritual Seeds

1. May all families obey these commandment of God: "You shall *not steal*," "You shall *not bear false witness* [lie]," and "You shall *not covet*" (emphasis added) (Exod. 20:15, 16, 17).
2. Be brave in being honest and telling the truth, even when friends do otherwise. Achan was brave to admit his sin.
3. "The eyes of the Lord are everywhere, keeping watch on the wicked and the good" (Prov. 15:3 NIV). God sees everything.
4. Remember, obedience to God's Word brings success and righteousness—disobedience brings consequences.

Mentor Your Replacement

Lesson 3: Joshua 22

Moses mentored Joshua to follow and obey God explicitly, and Joshua's last words reflect the impact Moses had on his life and ministry. Memorize Joshua's last words to the Hebrew nation; they are very similar to Moses's last sermon (see page 54). Joshua pleaded with the next generation to keep and follow God's commandments:

> *Only be very careful to observe the commandment and the law that Moses the servant of the* Lord *commanded you, to* **love the** Lord *your God, and* **to walk in all his ways** *and* **to keep his commandments and to cling to him [pray]** *and* **to serve him** *with all your heart and with all your soul* (emphasis added).
>
> —Josh. 22:5

Joshua's ministry was stellar until he failed to mentor his replacement, a godly leader for Israel. Godly leadership is the anchor that keeps a nation spiritually strong.

Plant Spiritual Seeds

1. Mentor your children to be godly parents, spouses, and citizens, thus blessing future generations. Aim for a domino effect with generation after generation mentoring their children to follow the Lord.

2. Encourage your children to *love the Lord, walk in His ways, keep His commandments, cling to Him,* and *serve Him.*
3. If you are in a place of service for the Lord, pray to God for a mentor who will continue your ministry. With the population increasing, you might even consider mentoring several people to continue your calling.
4. Choose godly leaders for your country.

Judges

The book of Judges begins after the deaths of Joshua and the elders. Israel had served the Lord as long as these men were alive, but after their deaths, the Israelites left the God of their fathers. Without a protégé to lead Israel, the country suffered greatly—especially spiritually. Joshua's final service for the Lord should have been to mentor a replacement.

For 350 years, the Israelites vacillated between trusting God and trusting idols. Each time they chose to worship idols, God punished them. Then Israel would plead for mercy, God would send a deliverer (a judge), and the Israelites would return to the God of their fathers, bringing peace for a season. Spiritually, Israel was on one big roller coaster for 350 years.

There were *15 judges* during this period. Some of the better-known judges who brought Israel back to God were Gideon, Deborah, and Samson.

God's Help Is Only a Prayer Away

Lesson: Judges 6, 8

Israel had become evil in the eyes of the Lord; therefore, God placed them in the hands of the Midianites for seven years. The Israelites even had to seek hiding places for protection. They finally cried out to God for help, and God chose Gideon to lead a miraculous battle against Midian.

Here is how it unfolded:

> And the angel of the LORD appeared to him [Gideon] and said to him, "The LORD is with you, O mighty man of valor." And Gideon said to him, "Please, my lord, if the LORD is with us, why then has all this happened to us? And where are all his wonderful deeds that our fathers recounted to us, saying, 'Did not the LORD bring us up from Egypt?' But now the LORD has forsaken us and given us into the hand of Midian."
> —Judg. 6:12–13

Without responding to his questions, the Lord told Gideon to go in His strength and save Israel. However, Gideon *doubted* he could save Israel. He argued that he was the least in his family, and his family was the weakest family in the tribe of Manasseh.

The Lord, through an angel, replied to Gideon, "I will be with you, and you will strike down all the Midianites, leaving none alive" (Judg. 6:16 NIV). Gideon needed verification that this was the angel of the Lord, so he asked the angel to stay and wait until he got back with an offering.

The angel of the Lord agreed, so Gideon left and returned with his offering. The angel asked Gideon to place his offering (meat and unleavened bread) on the rock and cover it with gravy, at which point the angel touched the offering with his staff. Fire from the staff completely consumed the meat and bread.

> *Then Gideon perceived that he was the angel of the* LORD. *And Gideon said, "Alas, O Lord* GOD! *For now I have seen the angel of the* LORD *face to face." But the* LORD *said to him, "Peace be to you. Do not fear; you shall not die."*
> —Judg. 6:22–23

Gideon still lacked faith because he asked the Lord for a sign as assurance that he could save Israel with God's help. He placed a fleece on the threshing floor and proclaimed that if the fleece were wet and the ground dry tomorrow, he would believe that, with the Lord's help, he could free Israel.

Early the next morning, Gideon dashed to the threshing floor and found the ground dry with enough dew on the fleece to make a bowl of water. Gideon did not want God to be upset with him, but he needed another sign before he could *really* believe. God patiently agreed. This time, Gideon wanted God to make the fleece dry and the ground wet.

It happened! The next morning, the fleece was dry, and dew covered the ground. Gideon now had the confirmation needed to fight the Midianites.

Early the next morning, Gideon and his men gathered at the Spring of Harod. The Midianites were north of them near Moreh. Since God wanted to win the battle for Gideon, He told Gideon that he had too many men, meaning that Gideon could win in his own strength. God did not want the men to boast about *their* winning the battle. Through a process of elimination, God cut Israel's troops from *32,000* men down to *300* men. With only a fraction of his original army, Gideon conceivably fought against *several hundred thousand* Midianites and Amorites and won. Their victory was miraculous!

God often chooses the weak to show His *strength*. Remember, Gideon's family was the weakest, and he was the least in his family. But with

Gideon's small army and *God's help*, Gideon delivered his people from the Midianites.

Plant Spiritual Seeds

1. If your child feels inadequate, doubtful, or scared, read Gideon's story (Judg. 6–8).
2. God's help is always sufficient. Train you children and grandchildren to seek God's help when things get tough and to always give God the glory when help arrives.

Ruth

In the book of Ruth, we meet a Moabite woman named Ruth who will be in the lineage of Jesus. She will marry a Hebrew man, Mahlon, son of Naomi and Elimelech. His family had come to Moab during a famine. Ruth became a lovely daughter-in-law to Naomi, and Naomi treated Ruth with kindness and love. They both lived exemplary lives.

Parents today need to mentor their children to become loving, caring husbands and wives who extend their love and concern to one another's families.

Naomi and Ruth: Exemplary Mother and Daughter-in-Law

Lesson: Ruth 1, 4

After Naomi and Elimelech moved to Moab with their sons, Mahlon and Chilion, Elimelech died, and then their two sons married Moabite girls, Ruth and Orpah. Ten years later, both of Naomi's sons died. Imagine her grief!

> She [Naomi] had heard in the fields of Moab that the LORD had visited his people and given them food. So she set out from the place where she was with her two daughters-in-law, and they went on the way to return to the land of Judah.
> —Ruth 1:6–7

The famine was over!

As Naomi, Orpah, and Ruth were on the road to Judah, Naomi tried to convince her two daughters-in-law to turn around and go back to their mothers' homes. Naomi recognized the girls' kindness toward her and granted them her blessings to return home and find other husbands.

Both girls still wanted to go with their mother-in-law to Judah. Finally, Orpah agreed to return to her family and kissed her mother-in-law goodbye. Ruth, however, clung to Naomi and pleaded:

> "Do not urge me to leave you or to return from following you. For where you go I will go, and where you lodge I will

> *lodge. Your people shall be my people, and your God my God. Where you die I will die, and there will I be buried. May the* LORD *do so to me and more also if anything but death parts me from you." And when Naomi saw that she was determined to go with her, she said no more.*
>
> —Ruth 1:16–18

After they arrived in Bethlehem, Naomi introduced Ruth to one of her relatives, Boaz. With the passing of time, Ruth and Boaz married, and the Lord blessed them with a son, whom they named Obed.

God did indeed have a good reason for Ruth to follow Naomi back to Judah. Ruth and Boaz's son, Obed, would become King David's grandfather, which placed Ruth in the lineage of Jesus: "Obed fathered Jesse, and Jesse fathered David" (Ruth 4:22).

Plant Spiritual Seeds

Encourage each of your married children to express a sincere concern and kindness for their spouse's family. A close relationship with in-laws will enrich their marriages and their lives. Their children will probably follow their examples, thereby creating a generational blessing.

1 Samuel

Samuel was born to a praying mother who at birth dedicated him to the Lord. When Samuel was a little boy, Hannah took him to the temple and literally gave him to Eli, the priest. Eli would become Samuel's mentor, and at Eli's death, Samuel would become Israel's priest.

After Eli's death and when Samuel was serving as Israel's priest, the people came to him and requested that Israel transition from a monotheistic government to a nation with an earthly king at the helm. Samuel prayed, and God told him to proceed with the transition.

Today, many countries have a king or president with self-serving ambitions as they lead their nations. Ideally, every country should seek a leader *who walks with the Lord and seeks His wisdom* as they make decisions affecting their nation and its people.

What is interesting, however, is that eventually our world will return to monotheism when Jesus returns as the King of kings and the Lord of lords. His return is called the Day of the Lord.

God Hears a Mother's Prayer

Lesson 1: 1 Samuel 1

As a woman of prayer, Hannah prayed fervently and made this vow to God:

> *O LORD of hosts, if you will indeed look on the affliction of your servant and remember me and not forget your servant, but will give to your servant a **son**, then I will **give him to the LORD** all the days of his life, and no razor shall touch his head* (emphasis added).
>
> —1 Sam. 1:11

Eli, the priest, observed Hannah's praying day after day. As she prayed in her heart, her lips moved, but no words came out. Suspecting she was drunk, Eli criticized her:

> *"Not so, my LORD," Hannah replied, "I am a woman who is deeply troubled. I have not been drinking wine or beer; I was pouring out my soul to the LORD. Do not take your servant for a wicked woman; I have been praying here out of great anguish and grief."*
>
> —1 Sam. 1:15–16 NIV

Have you ever fervently begged the Lord to answer a prayer? Be assured, God hears every prayer you have whispered and collects every tear that falls. Eli told Hannah, "Go in peace, and may the God of Israel grant you what you have asked of him" (1 Sam. 1:17 NIV). God did answer Hannah's prayer. When her son was born, she praised God and named him Samuel.

Plant Spiritual Seeds
1. Genuine prayers move the hand of God. Seek the Lord through prayer.
2. *Do not judge others.* Eli mistook Hannah's intense prayer for drunkenness. She was only pouring out her heart and soul to the Lord.
3. Fulfill your pledges. Hannah pledged to give God her son—and she did.
4. "The prayer of a righteous person is powerful and effective" (James 5:16 NIV). Seek to live a righteous life, and become a prayer warrior for others.

Dedicate Your Children to the Lord

Lesson 2: 1 Samuel 1

One of the sweetest newborn stories I have heard was of an aunt's recalling the day her nephew was born. After his birth, his grandfather anointed him with oil, praying he would walk with the Lord. He is now a successful college student, walking with the Lord and enjoying family and friends.

When each of your children or grandchildren is born, dedicate them to the Lord and pray that they will seek and discover God's will for their lives. Not everyone can become a preacher, but everyone is commanded to go and make disciples; every believer can and should serve the Lord. Raising daughters to become godly mothers affects the Lord's work. Jochebed raised Moses to have a heart for God, and Moses, through God, changed the course of Jewish history.

Hannah took Samuel to the temple because she had *pledged him to the Lord's work*. She said, "I have lent him to the Lord. As long as he lives, he is lent to the Lord" (1 Sam. 1:28).

Planting Spiritual Seed

1. Dedicate each of your children to the Lord.
2. Keep a separate journal for each of your children and record sweet, spiritual moments in their lives. What a treasure! For example, I asked our five-year-old son, "What is your favorite color?" He answered, "Red because that is the color of Jesus's blood."

You Reap What You Sow

Lesson 3: 1 Samuel 2

Throughout the Bible, there are amazing lessons about God's generosity toward us. The story of Samuel is a beautiful example.

> *But Samuel was ministering before the LORD—a boy wearing a linen ephod. Each year his mother made him a little robe and took it to him when she went up with her husband to offer the annual sacrifice. Eli would bless Elkanah and his wife, saying, "May the LORD give you children by this woman to take the place of the one she prayed for and gave to the LORD."*
>
> —1 Sam. 2:18–20 NIV

> *Indeed the LORD visited Hannah, and she conceived and bore three sons and two daughters. And the boy Samuel grew in the presence of the LORD.*
>
> —1 Sam. 2:21

You cannot outgive God. He is generous toward His children. Hannah and Elkanah generously gave their only child to the Lord. God blessed them with *five more children*.

Plant Spiritual Seeds

1. Be as generous toward God as He is toward you.
2. Teach generosity to your children from an early age.
3. Practice kindness toward others.
4. You always reap what you sow.

Always Obey God

Lesson 4: 1 Samuel 2

Obedience to God was and is the number one requirement for priests. Aaron, the first priest to serve the Lord, had four sons. Remember Aaron's two sons, Nadab and Abihu, who were consumed by fire because they disobeyed God? Their sin, disobedience, would be visited upon the third and fourth generations of Aaron's descendants.

The priests who followed Aaron were obedient priests who taught their sons to obey God. Yet years later when Eli served the Lord, he failed to teach his sons, Hophni and Phinehas, to obey God. Both Aaron and Eli excelled in their services to the Lord but failed as parents.

> *Now Eli was very old, and he kept hearing all that his sons were doing to all Israel, and how they lay with the women who were serving at the entrance to the tent of meeting. And he said to them, "Why do you do such things? For I hear of your evil dealings from all these people. No, my sons; it is no good report that I hear the people of the* Lord *spreading abroad. If someone sins against a man, God will mediate for him, but if someone sins against the* Lord*, who can intercede for him?" But they would not listen to the voice of their father, for it was the will of the* Lord *to put them to death.*
>
> —1 Sam. 2:22–25

After Eli told his sons they were not following God's laws, he closed his eyes when they closed their ears, and the boys continued their downward spiral of disobedience. Since Eli *did not teach* his sons to obey God, a prophet told Eli that his family would suffer the consequences, which would include the following:

- His family line would never have an old man.
- His two sons, Hophni and Phinehas, would both die on the same day.
- God would give his priestly line to a *new* family—Samuel (Hannah and Elkanah's son).

Because both Aaron and Eli failed to discipline their sons, these four young men had premature deaths. If only these two fathers had realized their boys' lives were at stake, they might have made a more concerted effort to discipline them.

Obituaries for each of these four boys could have read like this: Cause of Death: Disobedience.

Plant Spiritual Seeds

1. Teach your children self-discipline. Tell them what you expect them to do, and then step back and allow them to become responsible. If they are irresponsible, discipline them.
2. If your child faces discipline from outside the home, do not run interference. It is better to learn the hard way than to not learn at all.
3. Pray that your children's lives bring glory to God.

Pray for Your Children and Others

Lesson 5: 1 Samuel 2

We read in 1 Samuel 2:26, "Now the boy Samuel continued to grow both in stature and in *favor with the Lord* and also *with man*" (emphasis added). A similar verse in Luke 2:52 references Jesus: "And Jesus increased *in wisdom* and *in stature* and in *favor* with *God* and *man*" (emphasis added).

These two verses can translate into prayers for our children, spouses, friends, and us.

1. Prayer for children: "Lord, I pray that _____ will increase in wisdom (mentally) and stature (physically) and in favor with You, dear Lord (spiritually), and in favor with family and friends (socially)."

2. Prayer for adults: "Lord, I pray that _____ will increase in wisdom daily, will stay physically healthy, and will increase in favor with You, dear Lord, and in favor with family, friends, and associates."

Become prayer warriors for others. Prayer moves the hand of God. Here are some ways to remember prayer requests.

- A deacon in our church kept his prayer requests in a spiral notebook. He walked and prayed daily with his notebook in hand.
- Collect prayer requests on your cell phone.
- Write prayer requests on sticky notes, and place them where you frequent. A friend places her sticky notes around her mirror and prays as she prepares for the day.

- Choose to beseech the Lord *daily* on behalf of your family, friends, and country.

Plant Spiritual Seeds
1. Make a difference in the lives of others—pray for them.
2. Never forget that prayer moves the hand of God.
3. Make a concerted effort to nurture your children spiritually, mentally, physically, and socially.
4. "But when you pray, go into your room and shut the door and pray to your Father who is in secret. And your Father who sees in secret will reward you" (Matt. 6:6).
5. Through your example, encourage your children to pray for others.

Successful as Judges; Failure as Parents

Lesson 6: 1 Samuel 7–8

Samuel served the Lord beautifully as had Aaron and Eli. However, all three men failed as parents because they were *all* workaholics and spent little time parenting.

> *Samuel judged Israel all the days of his life. And he went on a circuit year by year to Bethel, Gilgal, and Mizpah. And he judged Israel in all these places. Then he would return to Ramah, for his home was there, and there also he judged Israel. And he built there an altar to the LORD.*
> —1 Sam. 7:15–17

Samuel's sons did not walk in the ways of the Lord. Instead, they were dishonest, accepted bribes, and disobeyed God's laws. When the elders of Israel recognized their lack of integrity, they approached Samuel and said, "Behold, you are old and your sons do not walk in your ways. Now appoint for us a king to judge us like all the nations" (1 Sam. 8:5). Israel wanted a human king to rule over them instead of the King of kings, God Almighty, their Heavenly Father.

The elders' request upset Samuel, so he prayed, and the Lord answered:

> *Obey the voice of the people in all that they say to you, for they have not rejected you, but they have rejected me from*

> *being king over them. According to all the deeds that they have done, from the day I brought them up out of Egypt even to this day, forsaking me and serving other gods, so they are also doing to you. Now then, obey their voice; only you shall solemnly warn them and show them the ways of the king who shall reign over them.*
>
> —1 Sam. 8:7–9

The first king of Israel will be Saul.

Why did Aaron, Eli, and Samuel fail as fathers? Eli had a generational curse on his family because his relative Aaron had failed as a parent. Possibly, Samuel failed because his mentor, Eli, failed to set a good example for him.

We can learn from Aaron's, Eli's, and Samuel's mistakes. Choose to give your children as much spiritual food as possible. Discipline them, and live exemplary lives before them. Your success will also affect your grandchildren's lives. A godly heritage is a priceless gift.

Plant Spiritual Seeds

1. Prioritize parenting. May each of your children and grandchildren reach their full potential spiritually, mentally, socially, and physically.
2. *Spiritual* development trumps mental, social, and physical development because it has eternal consequences. Never tire of planting spiritual seeds in your children's hearts.
3. Parents, be wise disciplinarians, and set godly examples.

Shun Evil, or Be Swept Away

Lesson 7: 1 Samuel 12

Throughout the ages, nations have risen only to be swept away. A country that stays in tune with God prospers and does well; however, any country that fails to follow God's commandments will *face destruction*. Samuel crowned Saul Israel's first king and then addressed the nation.

> *Only fear the Lord and serve him faithfully with all your heart. For consider what great things he has done for you. But if you still do wickedly, you shall be swept away, both you and your king.*
>
> —1 Sam. 12:24–25

It is clear that if a nation persists in doing evil, that country will be swept away.

Plant Spiritual Seeds

1. With your children, pray diligently for your country, its leaders, and those in authority.
2. If a country persists in doing evil, God will eventually sweep it away.
3. Strengthen your country by *sowing spiritual seeds everywhere*.

Inner Beauty Surpasses Outer Appearance

Lesson 8: 1 Samuel 16

Saul, Israel's first king, was handsome in every way, but he *did not walk with the Lord*. It was inevitable that King Saul would be *swept away*. God chose a man who had a heart for God from the house of Jesse to replace King Saul.

God sent Samuel to anoint the new king. The Lord had told Samuel, "Do not look on his appearance or on the height of his stature, because I have rejected him. For the LORD sees not as man sees: man looks on the outward appearance, but the LORD looks on the heart" (1 Sam. 16:7).

When Samuel arrived at the house of Jesse, he asked that each of Jesse's sons walk before him. Samuel thought several of the young men looked very kingly, but God kept reminding Samuel that He does not look on the outward appearance but on the heart. Then Jesse's youngest son, David, passed by. "And the LORD said, 'Arise, anoint him, for this is he'" (1 Sam. 16:12).

Israel's future king would be David, the great-grandson of Boaz and Ruth (Naomi's daughter-in-law, the Moabite). A future prophecy was evolving; Jesus would be born from the lineage of King David.

David's crowning took place years later after King Saul died.

Plant Spiritual Seeds

1. Encourage inner beauty. (Teach this lesson on Valentine's Day or before you teach the story of Samuel's anointing David as Israel's second king.) Buy a fancy Valentine box of candy, remove

the delicious candies, and put them into a brown paper sack. Put a handful of rocks into the fancy Valentine box. (If you are teaching a large number of children, buy individually wrapped candies for the brown paper sack, and enjoy the Valentine candies yourself.) To teach your children the importance of inner beauty, hold up the fancy Valentine box and teasingly ask, "What do you think is in this box?" "Candy!" Then hold up the brown paper sack, and ask, "Would you rather have what is in this sack?" They will invariably choose the fancy Valentine box. Open the Valentine box, and listen to their moans as they view the rocks. "This box is pretty on the outside, but rocks are not very tasty. Just because something is pretty on the outside does *not mean* it is pretty on the inside. Which is more important?" After they answer something like "inner beauty," pass out the candies in the paper sack, reminding them that God values inner beauty.[6]

2. God chose David because he exhibited the fruit of the spirit. Teach your children that inner beauty far surpasses outer appearances. Inner beauty (the fruit of the spirit) includes love, joy, peace, patience, kindness, goodness, faithfulness, gentleness, and self-control. It far surpasses outward appearances.

3. May we and our children have hearts for God and be *willing to do all His will.*

The David and Goliath Story
(Nothing Is Too Hard for God)

Lesson 9: 1 Samuel 17

At this point in history, Israel was at war with the Philistines. David, who had been anointed Israel's next king, was still just a shepherd boy, and his three brothers were serving in King Saul's army. One day, David's father asked him to check on his brothers and take them some food.

Early in the morning, David left his flock in the care of another shepherd and headed toward Israel's camp. He reached the camp as the army was moving into battle position, shouting their war cries. David dropped his things with the keeper of supplies and ran to the battlefield to see his brothers. As he was talking to his brothers, Goliath shouted that he wanted a man to fight. The Israelites became fearful. At that point, David learned that King Saul would give the man who killed Goliath great wealth, his daughter, and an exemption from paying taxes.

David told King Saul he would fight Goliath. Saul told him that he was just a boy, whereas the Philistine was a giant and an experienced fighter, and there was no way he could kill him.

David explained that he had taken good care of his father's sheep. If a lion or a bear attacked one of his sheep, he would overpower the animal and rescue the sheep from its mouth, even killing it, if necessary. David told King Saul he would treat Goliath as if he were a wild animal, and he would trust God to deliver him from the hand of this Philistine.

"Saul said to David, 'Go, and the LORD be with you!'" (1 Sam. 17:37).

David moved to the battle line and yelled this to the Philistine:

> *You come to me with a sword and with a spear and with a javelin, but I come to you in the name of the LORD of hosts, the God of the armies of Israel, whom you have defied. This day the LORD will deliver you into my hand, and I will strike you down and cut off your head. . . . For the battle is the LORD's, and he will give you into our hand.*
>
> —1 Sam. 17:45–47

Then David took a stone from his bag, put it into his slingshot, and hurled it straight into the Philistine's forehead. Immediately, Goliath fell to the ground. With *God's help,* David had won with only a slingshot and a stone.

After David killed Goliath, the Philistines turned and ran. The Israelites followed closely behind, shouting and killing them as they ran toward Gath and Ekron.

Plant Spiritual Seeds

1. Read the story of David and Goliath to your children (1 Sam. 17).
2. Teach your children that even though they are young, they can be *mighty* with God's help.
3. Seek God's help in all things. Nothing is impossible for Him (Luke 1:37).

Choose to Return Evil with Kindness

Lesson 10: 1 Samuel 24

After realizing David would become Israel's next king, Saul sought to kill David. While searching for David, Saul fell asleep in a cave where, unbeknownst to him, David and his men were hiding. The men encouraged David to kill the sleeping king, but David refused, choosing instead to cut off a corner of Saul's robe, which he later regretted.

Saul awoke and left the cave. Then David walked over to the cave's entrance, held up the corner of Saul's robe, and shouted at Saul that God had delivered him into his hands, but he spared Saul's life because he was God's anointed one. David then proclaimed, "May the LORD judge between me and you, may the LORD avenge me against you, but *my hand shall not be against you*" (emphasis added) (1 Sam. 24:12). David honored Saul because he was Israel's anointed king.

When David refrained from killing Saul, he exemplified God's command to *return evil with kindness* (see 1 Pet. 3:9).

Plant Spiritual Seeds

1. Return evil with kindness.
2. When another child takes your child's toy, hits, or bites, it is a moment to teach your child *not* to return evil with evil but to return evil with kindness.
3. Resist harming those who have harmed you; *instead, show kindness.*

Abigail Reciprocated Kindness with Kindness

Lesson 11: 1 Samuel 25

David and his men helped a wealthy man, Nabal, by protecting his sheep from raiders. But when Nabal was in a position to return David's kindness by feeding his hungry men, Nabal refused.

David said, "Surely in vain have I guarded all that this fellow has in the wilderness, so that nothing was missed of all that belonged to him, and he has returned me *evil for good*" (1 Sam. 25:21). Nabal's wife, Abigail, realized that Nabal had made this grave mistake and immediately took food to David and his men. Her kindness calmed David's anger, and he chose to overlook Nabal's ungraciousness.

When Abigail returned home and informed Nabal of her actions, his heart failed, and he died 10 days later.

> *When David heard that Nabal was dead, he said, "Praise be to the L*ORD*, who has upheld my cause against Nabal for treating me with contempt. He has kept his servant from doing wrong and has brought Nabal's wrongdoing down on his own head." Then David sent word to Abigail, asking her to become his wife.*
>
> —1 Sam. 25:39 NIV

Plant Spiritual Seeds
1. Do not return evil for kindness like Nabal did.
2. Reciprocate kindness with kindness as Abigail did.
3. Always overlook when others do you wrong.
4. Leave avenging to God as David did (thanks to Abigail).

2 Samuel

Second Samuel opens with the death of King Saul and the beginning of David's 40-year reign as king. Jerusalem becomes the capital of Israel, and David becomes known as a man with a heart for God. But no one is perfect, not even David. His life was not without blemishes. Though his sins weighed heavily upon his heart, he sought and received God's forgiveness. Scripture verifies that David received God's complete forgiveness. "I have found in David the son of Jesse a man after my heart, who will do *all* my will" (emphasis added) (Acts 13:22).

David's life demonstrated the truth that no matter how good a man is, he is still sinful. No one is perfect except Jesus, the Son of God. Through David, we learn that God is willing and able to forgive any sin.

Fulfill All Your Pledges

Lesson 1: 2 Samuel 9

David and Jonathan (Saul's son) had a brotherly love toward one another and pledged to always show kindness to each other's families. When Jonathan died, David remembered his pledge to his good friend and said, "Is there still anyone left of the house of Saul, that I may show him kindness for Jonathan's sake?" (2 Sam. 9:1). Saul's servant then told David that Jonathan had a son who was lame in both feet.

King David asked that Jonathan's son Mephibosheth be brought to the palace. When the young man arrived, he was frightened.

> "Don't be afraid," David said to him, "for I will surely show you kindness for the sake of your father Jonathan. I will restore to you all the land that belonged to your grandfather Saul, and you will always eat at my table."
> —2 Sam. 9:7 NIV

David showed generosity and kindness toward Mephibosheth.

Whenever you make a pledge (vow) to anyone, follow through with it. David exemplified true integrity when he faithfully fulfilled his pledge to his deceased friend Jonathan. Everyone needs to make a concerted effort to fulfill every pledge they make, even a small one such as returning a phone call, sending a recipe, or returning a borrowed item.

Plant Spiritual Seeds

1. With your children, make a vow to God to share a random act of kindness. Here are some suggestions:
   - Have your child draw a picture, and deliver it to an elderly neighbor.
   - Purchase coloring books and crayons to donate to a children's hospital.
   - Bake goodies, and deliver them to others.
2. May you and your family make a concerted effort to *fulfill all pledges (vows)* made to God and to others.

Confess and Seek Forgiveness for Your Sins

Lesson 2: 2 Samuel 12

The Lord saw King David who, in a weak moment, committed adultery with Bathsheba, the wife of Uriah, one of his soldiers. David then had Uriah put into harm's way to ensure his death. God revealed David's sins to Nathan, the priest, who then confronted David.

> David said to Nathan, "I have sinned against the LORD." And Nathan said to David, "The LORD also has put away your sin; you shall not die. Nevertheless, because by this deed you have utterly scorned the LORD, the child who is born to you shall die."
>
> —2 Sam. 12:13–14

David had sinned greatly, and it was probably very difficult for him to confess that sin. What a blessing that God forgives everyone who genuinely *seeks forgiveness* and *repents*. But they need to realize that there will still be consequences.

Below is David's prayer for forgiveness. May it also become your prayer for forgiveness.

> *Have mercy on me, O God,*
>   *according to your steadfast love;*
> *according to your abundant mercy*
>   *blot out my transgressions.*
> *Wash me thoroughly from my iniquity,*
>   *and cleanse me from my sin!*
> *For I know my transgressions,*
>   *and my sin is ever before me.*

> *Against you, you only, have I sinned*
> *   and done what is evil in your sight,*
> *so that you may be justified in your words*
> *   and blameless in your judgment.*
> *Behold, I was brought forth in iniquity,*
> *   and in sin did my mother conceive me.*
> *Behold, you delight in truth in the inward being,*
> *   and you teach me wisdom in the secret heart.*
> *Purge me with hyssop, and I shall be clean;*
> *   wash me, and I shall be whiter than snow.*
> *Let me hear joy and gladness;*
> *   let the bones that you have broken rejoice.*
> *Hide your face from my sins,*
> *   and blot out all my iniquities.*
> *Create in me a clean heart, O God,*
> *   and renew a right spirit within me.*
> *Cast me not away from your presence,*
> *   and take not your Holy Spirit from me.*
> *Restore to me the joy of your salvation,*
> *   and uphold me with a willing spirit.*
>
> —Ps. 51:1–12

After David prayed this prayer, he married Bathsheba. It is evident that God forgave David and Bathsheba, because God selected Solomon, another son born to David and Bathsheba, as the third king of Israel. David's complete forgiveness becomes even more evident when we realize that Jesus, God's Son, was from the lineage of David and Solomon. God certainly is a gracious and forgiving God!

Plant Spiritual Seeds

1. Teach your children to confess their wrongdoings—not to avoid consequences but to have a *clean heart.*
2. God expects repentance to follow forgiveness. Repentance is a commitment never to repeat a specific sin.
3. May we be as forgiving toward others as God is toward us.

Haughtiness Is a Sin
Lesson 3: 2 Samuel 24

King David ordered Joab, the commander of his army, to take a census of his fighting men within each tribe of Israel. Joab knew that *pride* prompted David to take this census, so he pleaded that the census be cancelled. David refused.

After completing the census, David was conscience-stricken and sought the Lord: "I have sinned greatly in what I have done. But now, O Lord, please take away the iniquity of your servant, for I have done very foolishly" (2 Sam. 24:10). David, like each of us, always had sin crouching at his door.

God prompted the prophet Gad to discipline David for his prideful actions. Gad gave King David the opportunity to choose his own discipline out of three possibilities. David selected the third one: "So the Lord sent a pestilence on Israel from the morning until the appointed time. And there died of the people from Dan to Beersheba 70,000 men" (2 Sam. 24:15).

David learned the hard way that God does not like haughtiness (pride). David evidently impressed this upon his son, King Solomon, because Solomon included haughtiness in his famous list of the seven things that God detests (Prov. 6:16–19).

Plant Spiritual Seeds

1. Teach humility in your home.
2. Do not be boastful.
3. Appreciate your God-given talents, but do not exhibit pride.
4. Sing "Oh Be Careful"[7] and shout out the words "no haughty eyes" (see page 180).

1 Kings

The book of 1 Kings begins at the end of King David's life and at the beginning of King Solomon's reign. In a dream, God gave Solomon an opportunity to ask for his heart's desire before he began his reign as Israel's third king. Solomon asked for and received great wisdom to better rule Israel. Since he knew right from wrong, he became a stellar king. In addition to wisdom, God gave him great wealth and honor. During the first 20 years of his reign, he built a beautiful temple for the Lord and a house for himself. This temple is still called Solomon's Temple.

Life was safe and secure during most of Solomon's 40-year reign. However, toward the end of his reign, he made a grave mistake when he sought foreign wives, most likely to benefit Israel politically. Sadly, however, many of those wives did not forgo idolatry, and Solomon accommodated their religion to the extent of participating in their idol worship.

Because Solomon *worshiped idols*, God would *strip 10 tribes* away from the family of David at Solomon's death. The 10 northern tribes would become the nation of Israel, and the remaining two tribes, Judah and Benjamin, would become the nation of Judah.

David's Last Words to Solomon

Lesson 1: 1 Kings 2

On his deathbed, David arranged time to talk with Solomon and prepare him to become a successful king. All fathers need to follow King David's example and give their children words of wisdom before they pass. Likewise, before your children leave home to face the real world, give them wise directives. David prepared Solomon to build a temple for the Lord.

David shared these powerful last words with Solomon:

> *I am about to go the way of all the earth. Be strong, and show yourself a man, and keep the charge of the LORD your God, walking in his ways and keeping his statutes, his commandments, his rules, and his testimonies, as it is written in the Law of Moses, that you may prosper in all that you do and wherever you turn, that the LORD may establish his word that he spoke concerning me, saying, "If your sons pay close attention to their way, to walk before me in faithfulness with all their heart and with all their soul, you shall not lack a man on the throne of Israel."*
>
> —1 Kings 2:2–4

> *Then David slept with his fathers and was buried in the city of David. . . . So Solomon sat on the throne of David his father, and his kingdom was firmly established.*
>
> —1 Kings 2:10, 12

Plant Spiritual Seeds

1. Emulate King David by choosing carefully the *last words* you speak or write to your children.
2. Before your children step out into the real world, give them directives to live a God-pleasing life.
3. While you are still mentally alert, write letters to each of your children and grandchildren, encouraging them to stay connected to their Heavenly Father, pleasing Him in every way. Remind them that it is their responsibility to lay a strong, spiritual foundation in the lives of the next generation by planting spiritual seeds and nurturing them to have hearts for God. Share your love for them, and then express appreciation for the lives they have lived. Your letters will be treasured.

Solomon's Wisdom Awed Everyone

Lesson 2: I Kings 3

In the introduction of 1 Kings, we read that Solomon asked for and received great wisdom from God to better rule the people of Israel. A story in 1 Kings stands out as an excellent example of Solomon's great wisdom. In Chapter 3, two women came to King Solomon seeking justice. They lived in the same house and had birthed babies three days apart.

One of the women complained:

> *This woman's son died in the night, because she lay on him. And she arose at midnight and took my son from beside me, while your servant slept, and laid him at her breast, and laid her dead son at my breast. When I rose in the morning to nurse my child, behold, he was dead. But when I looked at him closely in the morning, behold, he was not the child that I had borne.*
>
> —1 Kings 3:19–21

King Solomon replied with a striking decision.

> *Divide the living child in two, and give half to the one and half to the other. Then the woman whose son was alive said to the king, because her heart yearned for her son, "Oh, my lord, give her the living child, and by no means put him to death." But the other said, "He shall be neither mine nor yours; divide him." Then the king answered and said, "Give*

the living child to the first woman, and by no means put him to death; she is his mother." And all Israel heard of the judgment that the king had rendered, and they stood in awe of the king, because they perceived that the wisdom of God was in him to do justice.

—1 Kings 3:25–28

Plant Spiritual Seeds

1. Remember, *wisdom* means to know and do what is right.
2. Pray daily that your children will increase *in wisdom*, knowing and doing what is right, in stature (physically), and in favor with God (spiritually) and people (socially).
3. Wise choices create a good life. Poor choices make for a difficult life.

Fervently Pray for Your Country as King Solomon Prayed for Israel

Lesson 3: 1 Kings 8

King Solomon set a good example for us when he fervently prayed for Israel at the entrance of the newly completed temple. Below are excerpts from Solomon's prayer. Personalize his prayer by inserting your country and its people:

> *And listen to the plea of your servant and of your people Israel, when they pray toward this place. And listen in heaven your dwelling place, and when you hear, forgive. . . . When your people Israel are defeated before the enemy because they have sinned against you, and if they turn again to you and acknowledge your name and pray and plead with you in this house, then hear in heaven and forgive the sin of your people Israel and bring them again to the land that you gave to their fathers.*
>
> —1 Kings 8:30, 33–34

Regularly pray for your country. Gather a group of prayer warriors, and pray for specific needs in your country and for godly leadership. Here is a sample prayer for America:

> Hear my prayer, dear Heavenly Father, for America. May our people return to You, walk with You, and seek Your guidance daily. May we genuinely repent from our

wrongdoings and desire to follow Your ways. May we elect godly leaders for our country. We thank You, O Lord, for answering our prayers. In Jesus's name we pray, Amen.

Plant Spiritual Seeds
1. Remember, godly leadership is the anchor that keeps a nation strong.
2. Pray that God will bless your country.
3. Pray for Israel. May God bless Israel!
4. May the people of our country embrace their Heavenly Father.

2 Kings

While 1 Kings recorded the prosperous reign of King Solomon, 2 Kings unfortunately records the history of the rise and fall of Israel and Judah. They were now a divided kingdom because Solomon had practiced idolatry. Many prophets (preachers) encouraged these two countries to return to the Lord, but their pleas were ignored. The two main prophets during the divided kingdoms were Elijah and Elisha. Elijah mentored Elisha, but Elisha failed to mentor a replacement. That was not good.

Both nations failed to obey God's commandments, and eventually, they would both face deportation because of their ungodliness. The Israelites were deported 100 years prior to the Judeans. God allowed these deportations because His people would not self-correct and follow His ways.

Gehazi's Consequence for Lying: Leprosy

Lesson 1: 2 Kings 5

Naaman, the army commander for the king of Aram (present-day Syria), contracted leprosy and was advised by a young Jewish girl who worked for his wife to go to Israel and seek healing through Elisha. With no other options, he traveled to Samaria and found Elisha's house. Instead of Elisha coming out to pray for his healing, a messenger came out and told Naaman, "Go and wash in the Jordan seven times, and your flesh shall be restored, and you shall be clean" (2 Kings 5:10). Naaman was insulted, but finally he followed Elisha's instructions and was healed. To express his appreciation, Naaman offered gifts to Elisha, but Elisha refused to accept them. Instead, Elisha told Naaman, "Go in peace" (2 Kings 5:19).

However, Gehazi, Elisha's servant, devised a plan to take advantage of Naaman's generosity. Gehazi ran after Naaman, and when Naaman saw Gehazi running toward him, he stopped and got down from his chariot.

Gehazi, *lying* to Naaman, then explained, "My master has sent me to say, 'There have just now come to me from the hill country of Ephraim two young men of the sons of the prophets. Please give them a talent of silver and two changes of clothing'" (2 Kings 5:22). Naaman graciously gave Gehazi what he requested.

When Gehazi returned, Elisha asked where he had been. "And he said, 'Your servant went nowhere'" (2 Kings 5:25) (another lie).

GEHAZI'S CONSEQUENCE FOR LYING: LEPROSY

*But he [Elisha] said to him, "Did not my heart go when the man turned from his chariot to meet you? Was it a time to accept money and garments, olive orchards and vineyards, sheep and oxen, male servants and female servants? Therefore the **leprosy** of Naaman shall cling to you and to your descendants **forever**." So he went out from his presence a leper, like snow* (emphasis added).

—2 Kings 5:26–27

Lying is very serious. Solomon included lying on his list of the seven most detestable sins (Prov. 6:16–19). Jesus warned the people:

*I tell you that everyone will have to give account on the day of judgment **for every empty word they have spoken**. For by your words you will be acquitted, and by your words you will be condemned* (emphasis added).

—Matt. 12:36–37 NIV

Plant Spiritual Seeds

1. Explain to your children that lying is a slippery slope—once you lie, it becomes easier and easier to lie again.
2. Lying is a sin and can bring serious consequences. Gehazi lied twice, and his punishment was a lifetime of leprosy for him and his descendants. Wow!
3. If your child has trouble with lying, read the story of Gehazi (2 Kings 5).
4. God sees you wherever you are, including when you lie. Choose honesty, not lying.
5. There are always consequences when one lies (in either this life or the next).
6. Embellishment is a form of lying. Be very careful what you say. Do not exaggerate.
7. Sing with your children "Oh Be Careful," and shout out "never lie" (see page 180).

Israel Responded with Kindness toward Their Enemy

Lesson 2: 2 Kings 6

The Syrians were at war against Israel, unaware that God had enabled Israel to win each battle by informing Elisha where the Syrians were camped. Then Elisha would pass that information on to the king of Israel, creating a serious problem for the Syrians.

When the Syrian king realized Elisha was the informant, he sought to kill Elisha. "When the Syrians came down against him, Elisha prayed to the LORD and said, 'Please strike this people with blindness.' So he struck them with blindness in accordance with the prayer of Elisha" (2 Kings 6:18).

Elisha told the army of blind soldiers (who couldn't see that it was Elisha) that they were on the wrong road and in the wrong city. Then he volunteered to take them to Elisha. They accepted his offer, and Elisha led them to Samaria, the capital of Israel. In Samaria, Elisha prayed for the Lord to open their eyes, and He did. When the king of Israel saw them, he asked Elisha if he could kill the Syrians. Elisha answered, "You shall not strike them down. Would you strike down those whom you have taken captive with your sword and with your bow? Set bread and water before them, that they may eat and drink and go to their master" (2 Kings 6:22).

The king then prepared a great feast for the Syrian army. After this act of kindness, the Syrians stopped fighting Israel and returned home. "The Syrians did not come again on raids into the land of Israel" (2

Kings 6:23). Israel successfully won the battle because they responded with kindness toward their enemy.

Plant Spiritual Seeds

1. Using role-play, teach your children to be kind to friends who are unkind to them. Remember, we are to overlook when others wrong us. For example, if someone hits you, respond with something positive such as saying, "Let's go play ball."
2. Israel's kindness toward Syria ended the conflict between these two countries.
3. Encourage your children to always return evil with kindness.

Successes and Failures Mirror Our Spiritual Walks

Lesson 3: 2 Kings 20–21, 2 Chronicles 33, 36

King Hezekiah's success mirrored his walk with the Lord. As the king of Judah, he overcame generational curses. His father, Ahaz, had worshiped only idols, but he worshiped only God, and his life brought glory to God in every way. Even when he became afflicted with a terminal illness, he prayed to God for healing and was blessed with 15 additional years.

However, during those additional years, Hezekiah's spiritual walk became marred when he turned haughty. He was so proud of Judah's treasury that he smugly showed it to messengers from Babylon. The messengers were awed with Judah's beautiful treasures and desired to overtake Judah to confiscate them.

Besides showing haughtiness during that 15-year period, Hezekiah also fathered Manasseh, who became the king at the tender age of 12 and would reign 55 years in Jerusalem. Manasseh did not walk in the ways of the Lord. In fact, "he burned his son as an offering and used fortune-telling and omens and dealt with mediums and with necromancers [sorcerers]. He did much evil in the sight of the Lord, provoking him to anger" (2 Kings 21:6). The Lord said through the prophets that because of Manasseh's idolatry, He would bring so much disaster on Jerusalem and Judah that "the ears of everyone who hears of it will tingle" (2 Kings 21:12 NIV).

SUCCESSES AND FAILURES MIRROR OUR SPIRITUAL WALKS

After his father had lived such an exemplary life, why was Manasseh so sinful? Consider these possibilities:

- He was only 12 when his father died and was not fully grounded in the Lord.
- He was still in line for a generational curse because his grandfather, Ahaz, had embraced idol worship.

In 2 Chronicles, God spoke to Manasseh and the Judeans about their waywardness, but they ignored Him, and discipline became inevitable. God allowed the Assyrian army to bind Manasseh with hooks and chains and take him as a prisoner to Babylon where God would get his attention. There, Manasseh humbled himself and prayed to the Lord. "God was moved by his entreaty and heard his plea and brought him again to Jerusalem into his kingdom. Then Manasseh knew that the LORD was God" (2 Chron. 33:13).

After Manasseh repented, God was merciful and forgave him. Manasseh rebuilt the outer wall, *removed* the idols, *eliminated* idol worship, and *reinstated* the worship of God Almighty. Manasseh's response exemplified one who had truly repented (goes and sins no more).

Upon Manasseh's death, however, his son, Amon, did this:

> *And he did what was evil in the sight of the LORD, as Manasseh his father had done. Amon sacrificed to all the images that Manasseh his father had made, and served them. And he did not humble himself before the LORD, as Manasseh his father had humbled himself, but this Amon incurred guilt more and more.*
>
> —2 Chron. 33:22–23

Manasseh received forgiveness, yet his family's generational curse led Judah closer to her 70-year Babylonian captivity.

Plant Spiritual Seeds

1. Pray fervently for your children, and plant many spiritual seeds in their lives.

2. Do not flaunt your possessions; instead, be humble and grateful.
3. Choose to walk with the Lord. Manasseh sinned yet finished strong because he repented and returned to his Heavenly Father. Forgiveness is available to everyone.
4. Manasseh's son, Amon, followed *only the undesirable practices of his father*.
5. Encourage your children to follow *only the positive examples they see in your life*.
6. Do not create generational curses for your family. They are very difficult to overcome.
7. Successes and failures mirror our spiritual walks. Stay spiritually strong!
8. Like God, give others a second chance.

1 Chronicles

The book of 1 Chronicles was probably written by Ezra during the Babylonian captivity. It describes the Jewish history during the reigns of King Saul and King David, presenting history from a religious point of view.

This book inspired the Jews returning from their Babylonian captivity to remember their extraordinary spiritual heritage. They needed much encouragement as they began rebuilding their nation from the inside out.

Prepare Children for Success

Lesson: 1 Chronicles 22

Those returning from Babylonia needed to follow God's directives in order to successfully rebuild Solomon's Temple. King David had spoken encouraging words to Solomon as he prepared to build the original temple, so the author of 1 Chronicles wisely chose to read those words to the returnees to inspire the rebuilding of Solomon's Temple.

Pray David's encouraging words to Solomon over your child or over anyone who is stepping out into the real world:

> *Now, my son, the Lord be with you, so that you may succeed in building the house of the Lord your God, as he has spoken concerning you. Only, may the Lord grant you discretion and understanding, that when he gives you charge over Israel you may keep the law of the Lord your God. Then you will prosper if you are careful to observe the statutes and the rules that the Lord commanded Moses for Israel. Be strong and courageous. Fear not; do not be dismayed.*
> —1 Chron. 22:11–13

It was David's pleasure to gather materials and seek workmen for Solomon.

> *With great pains I have provided for the house of the Lord 100,000 talents of gold, a million talents of silver, and bronze and iron beyond weighing, for there is so much of*

PREPARE CHILDREN FOR SUCCESS

> *it; timber and stone, too, I have provided. To these you must add. You have an abundance of workmen: stonecutters, masons, carpenters, and all kinds of craftsmen without number, skilled in working gold, silver, bronze, and iron. Arise and work! The L*ORD *be with you!*
> —1 Chron. 22:14–16

After the returnees listened to all David had done to help Solomon build the original temple, they had a better grasp of what it would take to *rebuild* Solomon's Temple.

We as parents need to prepare our children for success as well. Do enough to get them going in the right direction but not so much that they remain dependent on you. Our son-in-law Scott received wise advice from his dad when preparing for his first summer job. As a teenager, Scott asked his dad to buy him a motorcycle. His dad replied, "Earn the money and buy it yourself, Son." Scott thought that sounded like an impossible feat and asked how he could ever earn enough money.

"Well, I see many lawns in the neighborhood that need mowing," his dad said. "You could mow lawns." Scott agreed and scouted the neighborhood for customers. Excited that a number of neighbors had committed to using his lawn service, he returned home and headed straight to the garage to get the family's lawnmower. His dad stopped him and asked, "What are you doing?"

"I'm getting the lawnmower so I can start mowing."

"Not with *my* mower you aren't, Son," his dad replied. "But you can fix the broken one behind the garage, if you wish." Then the two of them took apart the old mower, cleaned each part, bought needed parts, and put everything back together. Scott was now open for business. And having built his mower from scratch, he was well able to maintain it.

What a happy day it was when Scott bought his first motorcycle with his own hard-earned money. He treasures the lessons he learned from his dad.

Prepare boys to meet the physical needs of their families. God has given each person specific talents and abilities. May your son seek

God's direction for his life. Even though it often takes two incomes to meet the needs of a family, always prioritize the needs of your children over jobs. Mothers are by nature more nurturing than fathers. All little girls need a doll to nurture and love to prepare for motherhood.

Together, parents need to sit down and discuss how best to meet their children's spiritual, physical, mental, and social needs. Children are gifts from God, and their needs should supersede parents' desires.

Pray fervently that *the hand of God will be on your children* as they live their lives.

Plant Spiritual Seeds

1. Observe your children, and take note of their God-given talents. Help them discover possible occupations that complement their talents.
2. Prepare your children for success.

2 Chronicles

The book of 2 Chronicles is a chronicle of Judah's history extending from the original building of Solomon's Temple through the Babylonian captivity and continuing until the Judeans resettled the Holy Land with plans to rebuild Solomon's Temple.

We will focus on six kings, all descendants of King David, and determine how their lives provide parenting lessons for us today. Five of the six kings had the potential of becoming exemplary kings. Only two succeeded. The sixth king failed because he had too many generational curses.

1. King Solomon encouraged the Israelites to pray, repent, and seek forgiveness whenever they sinned. However, toward the end of his reign, he *tarnished* his reign by embracing idolatry.
2. King Abijah, *an exemplary king*, trusted and obeyed his Heavenly Father.
3. King Asa followed the example of his father, King Abijah, until his 36th year when he *tarnished* his reign by seeking Syria's help instead of God's help.
4. King Joash was *doomed* from the beginning because he had too many generational curses.
5. King Uzziah put his trust in God and won many battles. He was a great king until pride *tarnished* his reign.
6. King Josiah, *an exemplary king*, was passionate about knowing and obeying the Word of God.

Rulers and presidents definitely affect the spiritual welfare of their countries.

King Solomon: "Sinners: Pray, Repent, and Seek Forgiveness" (Tarnished)

Lesson 1: 2 Chronicles 7

Sin weakens a family and eventually a nation if it permeates into the fabric of a multitude of families. King Solomon made a positive impact on Israel when he encouraged the people to pray, repent, and seek God's forgiveness.

Upon the completion of the temple, King Solomon dedicated it to God. At the dedication, God appeared to Solomon and said this:

> *I have heard your prayer and have chosen this place for myself as a house of sacrifice. When I shut up the heavens so that there is no rain, or command the locust to devour the land, or send pestilence among my people,* **if my people who are called by my name humble themselves, and pray and seek my face and turn from their wicked ways, then I will hear from heaven and will forgive their sin and heal their land.** *Now my eyes will be open and my ears attentive to the prayer that is made in this place. For now I have chosen and consecrated this house that my name may be there forever. My eyes and my heart will be there for all time* (emphasis added).
>
> —2 Chron. 7:12–16

Many countries have prayed these verses to move their people back into fellowship with God. Anyone living in sin can do likewise.

King Solomon reigned over all Israel for 40 years. God repeatedly warned him to stay faithful to Him.

> *But if you turn aside and forsake my statutes and my commandments that I have set before you, and go and serve other gods and worship them, then I will pluck you up from my land that I have given you.*
>
> —2 Chron. 7:19–20

Sadly, King Solomon became *tarnished* when he stooped to worshiping idols. As already mentioned, Solomon repented, but his country still suffered consequences. At Solomon's death, God removed the tribes of Judah and Benjamin from the nation of Israel and created a new nation called Judah. Solomon's son Rehoboam become Judah's first king.

Plant Spiritual Seeds

1. Sin always results in consequences.
2. Follow King Solomon's advice. When you sin, pray, repent, and seek forgiveness.
3. Pray for God's eyes and heart to always be in your home, presiding over your family.
4. Teach your children that no one is above God's laws and commandments, not even kings.

King Abijah: "Rely on the Lord, Your God" (Exemplary)

Lesson 2: 2 Chronicles 13

When King Rehoboam died, his son Abijah became Judah's second king. War between Judah and Israel was on the horizon. King Abijah stood on Mount Zemaraim and rebuked Israel and King Jeroboam for their rebellion and idolatry.

> *But as for us, the Lord is our God, and we have not forsaken him. . . . For we keep the charge [commandments] of the Lord our God, but you have forsaken him. Behold, God is with us. . . . O sons of Israel, do not fight against the Lord, the God of your fathers, for you cannot succeed.*
> —2 Chron. 13:10–12

Israel chose to fight. What do you suppose happened? Judah, with only 400,000 men, won over Israel's 800,000 men, inflicting 500,000 fatalities on Israel's army.

King Abijah knew that God had provided the victory.

> *Thus the men of Israel were subdued at that time, and the men of Judah prevailed, because they **relied** on the Lord, the God of their fathers* (emphasis added).
> —2 Chron. 13:18

KING ABIJAH: "RELY ON THE LORD, YOUR GOD" (EXEMPLARY)

Judah's *spiritual strength* enabled her army to win the battle. Spiritual strength is needed to fight any battle. Like King Abijah, our children need to *rely on God* and stand strong during adversities in order to succeed.

Abijah, *an exemplary king*, died with honor, but Israel's King Jeroboam never regained power. The Lord struck him down, and he died. He reaped what he had sown.

Plant Spiritual Seeds

1. Parents, when you set an example for your children and lean on God's strength in times of trouble, your children will probably emulate you when they are weak.
2. Pray when your children face strongholds, tests, or trials. Here is an exemplary prayer: "Help us, O Lord our God, for *we rely on You*, and in Your name we have come against _____. Lord, You are our God; do not let _____ prevail against us. In Jesus's name we pray, Amen."

King Asa: "Always Trust God!" (Tarnished)

Lesson 3: 2 Chronicles 14, 16

After King Abijah died, his son, Asa, came to the throne and followed his father's godly example. "He commanded Judah to seek the LORD, the God of their ancestors, and to obey his laws and commands" (2 Chron. 14:4 NIV). King Asa relied on the Lord when Judah went into battle against the Ethiopians, and his prayer is a model prayer for any family.

> *O LORD, there is none like you to help, between the mighty and the weak. Help us, O LORD our God, for we rely on you, and in your name, we [army of 580,000] have come against this multitude [army of a million]. O LORD, you are our God; let not man prevail against you.*
>
> —2 Chron. 14:11

God answered his prayer, and Judah struck down the Ethiopians. He again helped a smaller nation win against a larger nation—like father, like son. Judah would enjoy peace for 35 years, but in Asa's 36th year, *he did not seek the Lord's help* when Israel threatened Judah. He sought the help of Syria to resolve the conflict. Five years later, King Asa died a *tarnished king* because *he trusted Syria instead of God.*

Everyone should seek and trust God throughout their lives. Our Heavenly Father is available 24/7.

Plant Spiritual Seeds

1. Be a positive example for your children. Whenever a problem occurs, seek your Heavenly Father's help to calm your storm.
2. Keep communications open between you and your children so they will share their needs and concerns with you. Together, seek the Lord's help and His wisdom.
3. If you have a need, ask your child(ren) to pray for you. May your family react to adversities as a team and *always* with prayer, trusting the Lord.

King Joash: "Do Not Underestimate Generational Curses" (Doomed)

Lesson 4: 2 Chronicles 21–22, 24

When Joash's grandfather, King Jehoram, was crowned king of Judah, he killed all his brothers to secure his kingship. He then brought additional curses on his heirs when he married Athaliah, the wicked, idol-worshiping daughter of Israel's evil King Ahab and Queen Jezebel. After Jehoram married Athaliah, he embraced idolatry and followed Israel's evil ways. The Prophet Elijah even wrote to King Jehoram, announcing that Judah would reap destruction because of his ungodly walk and his decision to worship idols. Elijah then prophesied that Jehoram would experience a painful death. "He departed with no one's regret" (2 Chron. 21:20).

After King Jehoram died, his youngest son, Ahaziah, became the new king of Judah. "He also walked in the ways of Ahab, for *his mother* [Athaliah] *was his counselor in doing wickedly*" (emphasis added) (2 Chron. 22:3). As king, Ahaziah lived only a year before dying on the battlefield. Afterward, his mother, Athaliah, attempted to annihilate all the royal heirs in the house of Judah with plans to rule as the Queen of Judah. But unbeknownst to Queen Athaliah, Ahaziah's half-sister took baby Joash and hid him in God's temple. So while Queen Athaliah was ruling Judah, within the temple, God was protecting Joash and giving his aunt and uncle (the priest Jehoiada) an opportunity to nurture him in the ways of the Lord.

KING JOASH: "DO NOT UNDERESTIMATE GENERATIONAL CURSES"

When Joash was seven, Priest Jehoiada initiated plans to overthrow Queen Athaliah. He succeeded, and Joash became the King of Judah. Besides being young, Joash had to contend with many generational curses.

King Joash honored God during his initial reign because Priest Jehoiada directed him in the ways of the Lord. However, after Jehoiada's death, King Joash became spiritually weak, as did his country. The people abandoned the temple and began worshiping idols. God's anger arose against Judah.

Priest Zechariah, the son of Jehoiada, urged the people to repent, saying, "Thus says God, 'Why do you break the commandments of the Lord, so that you cannot prosper? Because you have forsaken the Lord, he has forsaken you'" (2 Chron. 24:20). King Joash, angered by Zechariah's words, ordered that he be *stoned to death* in the courtyard of the Lord's temple. This was a bad decision. Joash was accountable to God and died shortly thereafter.

King Joash was practically *doomed to fail* because of his many generational curses.

Plant Spiritual Seeds

1. Plant an abundance of spiritual seeds in the hearts of those children who contend with generational curses.
2. King Joash's seven years of spiritual nourishment were insufficient to combat the deep-seeded generational curses.
3. Joash depended on Jehoiada, not God, for his spiritual strength.
4. May your children be spiritually strong *before* they leave your home.

King Uzziah: "Be Careful, Pride Goes before a Fall" (Tarnished)

Lesson 5: 2 Chronicles 26

After Joash's death, "all the people of Judah took Uzziah, who was sixteen years old, and made him king instead of his father Amaziah" (2 Chron. 26:1). Unlike Joash, Uzziah had learned from Priest Zechariah that "as long as he sought the Lord, God made him prosper" (2 Chron. 26:5). Therefore, King Uzziah successfully won battles against the Philistines, the Arabs, and the Meunites and rebuilt many towns. "His fame spread even to the border of Egypt, for he became very strong" (2 Chron. 26:8). However, Uzziah's power led to pride, which became his downfall.

Feeling indestructible, King Uzziah entered the temple of the Lord and burned incense, a task permitted only by the holy priests. Azariah and 80 other priests then confronted the king:

> It is not for you, Uzziah, to burn incense to the Lord, but for the priests, the sons of Aaron, who are consecrated to burn incense. Go out of the sanctuary, for you have done wrong, and it will bring you no honor from the Lord God.
> —2 Chron. 26:18

When King Uzziah became enraged at the priests' reprimands, leprosy suddenly broke out on his forehead. The priests quickly escorted him out of the temple, realizing that the Lord had afflicted him with leprosy. "King Uzziah was a leper to the day of his death, and being a leper lived in a separate house, for he was excluded from the house of the LORD" (2 Chron. 26:21). Uzziah's son Jotham replaced him as king.

Uzziah had been a good king until pride set in. He should have chosen to always live an exemplary life, but instead, he allowed his position and his power to fill him with pride.

Unfortunately, Uzziah is remembered as a *tarnished king*.

Plant Spiritual Seeds

1. Be careful! Pride often precedes a fall.
2. Instead of being prideful, be humble.
3. Respond to your children's successes by giving God the glory:
   - For example, if your child played well in a soccer game, respond, "God gave you great agility!"
   - If your child exhibits kindness toward another, respond, "It is obvious God gave you a kind spirit because you were so nice to _____."
4. Tell your children frequently, "God loves you," and remind them to let their light *shine for Him all day, every day*.

King Josiah: "Read and Obey the Word of the Lord" (Exemplary)

Lesson 6: 2 Chronicles 34

King Josiah, another *exemplary king*, learned the importance of reading and obeying God's Word, especially the Ten Commandments. While repairing the house of the Lord in Jerusalem, Hilkiah the priest found the Book of the Law (the first five books of the Bible written by Moses) and gave it to Shaphan, King Josiah's secretary, who then read it to the king.

Upon hearing the words of the law, King Josiah tore his robe and wept in despair, realizing the kings who had come before him had not followed the laws of God. Then he gathered the elders of Jerusalem and all the Judeans in the temple where he read them the Book of the Law.

> *And the king stood in his place and made a covenant before the Lord, to walk after the Lord and to keep his commandments and his testimonies and his statutes, with all his heart and all his soul, to perform the words of the covenant that were written in this book.*
>
> —2 Chron. 34:31

King Josiah next had everyone in Jerusalem commit to the ways of the Lord. He removed the idols their ancestors had set up throughout the land and purged the land of idolatry. As long as King Josiah lived, the people faithfully followed the Lord.

Josiah died an *exemplary king* and was mourned by all.

Plant Spiritual Seeds

1. As a family, read the Bible, and find messages from God.
2. Godly leadership makes a big difference.
3. Pray for the people in other countries who can neither read their Bibles nor openly live out their faith. Be thankful for your religious freedoms.
4. Be sure your children know the Word so they can keep the Word.
5. May each generation accept the responsibility to teach the next generation God's Word.

Ezra

The book of Ezra begins at the end of Judah's 70-year exile in Babylonia. The Persians now govern Babylonia, and King Cyrus, a pagan, sits on the throne. "Thus says Cyrus king of Persia: The LORD, the God of heaven, has given me all the kingdoms of the earth, and he has charged me to *build him a house at Jerusalem, which is in Judah*" (emphasis added) (Ezra 1:2). Through God's divine providence, King Cyrus encouraged a group of Jewish believers to return to Judah to rebuild Solomon's Temple.

But many problems would ensue, creating delays in the timely rebuilding of the temple.

Prayers Move the Hand of God

Lesson: Ezra 8

Years later, the new king of Persia, King Artaxerxes, allowed a second group of Jewish believers to leave for Judah. Ezra, a priest from the lineage of Aaron, led this group. It concerned him that the people in Judah had intermarried and were ignoring the ways of the Lord. His purpose for traveling to Jerusalem was to teach the Judeans the decrees and laws of Moses.

Ezra proclaimed a fast and asked the Judeans to pray for safe travel before he sought permission from King Artaxerxes to travel to Jerusalem.

> *For I [Ezra] was ashamed to ask the king for a band of soldiers and horsemen to protect us against the enemy on our way, since we had told the king, "The hand of our God is for good on all who seek him, and the power of his wrath is against all who forsake him."*
>
> —Ezra 8:22

The king graciously granted permission for their travel to Jerusalem, giving them silver and gold as well as a multitude of gifts for the temple. Others in Babylon also sent offerings to those living in Judah. God answered their prayers for safe travel, and the entire group arrived in Jerusalem without any incidents along the way.

Plant Spiritual Seeds

1. Prayer is a vital element when it comes to serving the Lord. Pray before each project, pray during each project, and pray after each project.
2. Ask that the hand of God be on you and your children and grandchildren. Pray the following prayer daily: Lord I pray that _____ is in your will today. Please hold _____ by your right hand, and give _____ success and direction.
3. God's hand protected Ezra's group, and His hand can protect us and our children when problems arise.

Nehemiah

After the first two groups had resettled in Judah, Nehemiah, a Jewish cupbearer for King Artaxerxes, asked if he could lead a third and final group back to Jerusalem with the intention of rebuilding the city's wall and gates. King Artaxerxes granted Nehemiah's request.

Nehemiah Sought and Received God's Help

Lesson 1: Nehemiah 1–2, 4, 6

In Susa (Babylon), the capital of Persia, Nehemiah talked with his brother Hanani and others who had come from Judah and learned that the Jews in Jerusalem were greatly troubled because the walls of their city had been destroyed and their gates burned. Upon hearing this, Nehemiah wept. For days he mourned, fasted, and prayed to God on behalf of Jerusalem and its needs.

He was determined to rebuild Jerusalem's wall and gates, but first he needed King Artaxerxes' permission. He asked God to grant him favor with King Artaxerxes.

Read Nehemiah's prayer aloud. It is truly a model prayer for anyone seeking a request from the Lord.

> *O LORD, let your ear be attentive to the prayer of your servant, and to the prayer of your servants who delight to fear your name, and give success to your servant today, and grant him mercy in the sight of this man.*
>
> —Neh. 1:11

"The king granted me what I asked, for the good hand of my God was upon me" (Neh. 2:8). King Artaxerxes gave Nehemiah letters for safe passage to Judah as well as a letter to Asaph, the keeper of the king's forest, to provide the wood needed to rebuild the gates, the wall, and their future homes.

After Nehemiah arrived safely in Jerusalem, he faced many problems rebuilding the city's wall and gates, including serious threats of physical harm. Because of the threats, half of his men worked on the walls while the other half guarded the workers.

Success required perseverance and physical strength. Nehemiah continuously reminded the men, "The God of heaven will make us prosper" (Neh. 2:20). God did give them success; they completed the wall in just 52 days, even while facing adversities.

Plant Spiritual Seeds

1. Follow Nehemiah's example when facing problems and difficulties: pray, fast, and repent before seeking God's help.
2. Praise your Heavenly Father when He gives you success or helps you resolve problems.
3. Seek wisdom (to know and do what is right). Remember, obedience to God brings success.

To Experience Revival, Read His Word

Lesson 2: Nehemiah 8–9

After completing the wall, the people in Jerusalem returned to God and became spiritually strong. They listened attentively to Ezra as he read the Book of the Law from daybreak until noon. "And Ezra blessed the Lord, the great God, and all the people answered, 'Amen, Amen,' lifting up their hands" (Neh. 8:6).

After the people listened to the Book of the Law, they worshiped the Lord and wept. Those convicted of their sins repented and received forgiveness. Nehemiah told them, "Go and enjoy choice food and sweet drinks, and send some to those who have nothing prepared. This day is holy to our Lord. Do not grieve, for the joy of the Lord is your strength" (Neh. 8:10 NIV). What a sacred day for Nehemiah, Ezra, the Levites, and all the Judeans who participated!

Everyone's faith continued to grow as they listened to the Word and recalled the miracles Israel had experienced. They remembered the day when God parted the Red Sea, allowing His people to cross over on dry ground. They remembered when God led the people with a cloud by day and a pillar of fire by night, and they remembered when God sustained them in the desert for 40 years.

What a revival these people experienced! If you believe your life might not be pleasing to your Heavenly Father, seek repentance, and return to Him like these Judeans did.

Plant Spiritual Seeds

1. Strengthen children spiritually. Read Bible stories to your younger children, and purchase age-appropriate Bibles and devotional books for older children.
2. If you or your family has slid backward in your relationship with your Heavenly Father, return to church, listen to His Word, read His Word, repent of your sins, and renew your walk with Him.
3. Allow the Good Shepherd to remold you and use you daily.

Esther

"God protects His people" is the theme of Esther. Even after three groups of Judeans returned to Judah, a large number remained in Persia (Babylonia). God orchestrated a plan to protect those still living in Persia through the life of an orphaned Jewish girl named Esther.

Speak Up Boldly for the Lord

Lesson: Esther 3–4

Haman, a high official in the Persian (Babylonian) government, became angry with a man named Mordecai, who happened to be Queen Esther's cousin, because he refused to bow down to him. In anger, Haman influenced King Xerxes to sign a proclamation to annihilate all the Jewish people still living in Persia. King Xerxes signed the proclamation, unaware that his own wife, Queen Esther, was Jewish.

Mordecai sent word to Esther of King Xerxes's proclamation and pleaded with her to approach the king and intervene on behalf of the Jewish people. Here is Mordecai's reply to her:

> *Do not think to yourself that in the king's palace you will escape any more than all the other Jews. For if you keep silent at this time, relief and deliverance will rise for the Jews from another place, but you and your father's house will perish.*
>
> —Esther 4:13–14

Esther became frightened, knowing that she would be killed if the king did not acknowledge her by raising his scepter. She needed God's help.

So Esther asked Mordecai to gather all the Jews in Susa and have them fast and pray for three days and nights for her. She and her servants would do likewise. Esther replied, "Then I will go to the king, though it is against the law, and if I perish, I perish" (Esther 4:16).

After many people had prayed and fasted, Esther approached King Xerxes. When the king raised his scepter to give permission for her to speak, Esther breathed a sigh of relief and boldly interceded on behalf of the Jewish nation.

King Xerxes chose to protect the Jewish people and ordered Haman hanged for his plot against the Jews.

Plant Spiritual Seeds

1. Teach your children to *boldly speak out* for the Lord and His people, like Queen Esther.
2. Spend time praying and fasting with your family before making significant decisions.

Job

God permitted Satan to test Job's spiritual strength by bringing trials and tribulations upon him. This testing began with the deaths of his seven sons; three daughters; 7,000 sheep; 3,000 camels; 500 yoke of oxen; and 500 donkeys as well as the deaths of his servants—all in rapid succession. God, however, protected Job's wife.

Through all Job's trials and tribulations, he stood firm. Then Satan asked God if he could tempt Job physically. God gave permission with the stipulation that Satan could not take Job's life. Satan agreed and then afflicted Job with painful sores over his entire body.

Friends came to check on him and found him unrecognizable because his sufferings were so great. They wept and stayed with him for seven days. They were full of reasons for his sufferings, including his need to seek forgiveness for his wrongdoings. They questioned his walk with the Lord. Job responded:

> *For I know that my Redeemer lives, and at the last he will stand upon the earth. And after my skin has been thus destroyed, yet in my flesh I shall see God, whom I shall see for myself, and my eyes shall behold, and not another. My heart faints within me!*
> —Job 19:25–27

Even after physical attacks, Job stood firm.

After Job's three older friends tried unsuccessfully to explain the reasons behind Job's horrendous sufferings, a fourth friend, Elihu, burned with anger and burst forth with five reasons Job should be declared righteous.

Elihu's response to Job's sufferings provides us with five parenting lessons.

Listen with Your Heart—Be an Active Listener

Lesson 1: Job 34

Elihu speaks:

> *Hear my words, you wise men; listen to me, you men of learning. For the ear tests words as the tongue tastes food.*
> —Job 34:2–3 NIV

With insight from God, Elihu explained to Job's friends that they should have listened more carefully to Job and sought God's thoughts before they spoke whatever came into their foolish minds.

Plant Spiritual Seeds

1. Train your children to listen carefully while others speak. Become an active listener, responding appropriately.
2. Take your children outside and tell them to shut their eyes and listen to all the sounds around them. Ask, "What do you hear?" Compliment their listening skills when they identify a sound.
3. Give family and friends your full attention—*listen with your heart.*
4. Read to your children, and ask them questions about what you have read.

Live Righteously, and Please Your Heavenly Father

Lesson 2: Job 34

Elihu speaks again:

> *Therefore, hear me, you men of understanding: far be it from God that he should do wickedness, and from the Almighty that he should do wrong. . . . Of a truth, God will not do wickedly, and the Almighty will not pervert justice.*
>
> —Job 34:10, 12

Job's lifestyle was not responsible for his sufferings. He was righteous in the eyes of the Lord, and his pain and sufferings were not due to unrighteous living. His lifestyle pleased his Heavenly Father.

Plant Spiritual Seeds

1. Even through sufferings, live a God-pleasing life.
2. Strive to always do what is right, and live righteously like Job.

Do Not Judge Others—Comfort Them

Lesson 3: Job 34

Elihu said to Job:

> *He [God] repays everyone for what they have done; he brings on them what their conduct deserves.*
> —Job 34:11 NIV

Struggles are not always indicative of our walks with the Lord. Might God allow struggles for our own good? Yes. Was this true in Job's case? Yes.

We should not judge others who are passing through difficult times but understand that those who willfully do wrong are accountable to God for their actions.

Only God knows our hearts and intentions. We are all accountable to Him and should *never judge others*.

Plant Spiritual Seeds

1. Instead of judging those who are going through trials, offer empathy, compassion, and encouragement—not judgment.
2. Remember, God prunes those who walk with Him to increase their productivity.
3. Since we are accountable to God for our walks in life, strive to not do anything wrong.

He Sees Our Every Step—Let Your Light Shine for Him

Lesson 4: Job 34

His eyes are on the ways of mortals; he sees their every step.
—Job 34:21 NIV

If God sees even a sparrow when it falls to the ground, we know that He sees everything we do, day and night. Everyone is accountable for their walks.

Plant Spiritual Seeds
1. Remind your children to live lives that shine brightly and bring honor to their Heavenly Father and to their parents.
2. God is available to listen to your prayers every minute of every day.
3. Memorize this: "His eyes are on the ways of mortals; he sees their every step" (Job 34:21 NIV).

Trust God in All Situations—He Is in Control

Lesson 5: Job 36–37

It is easy to picture Elihu standing a little taller and talking a little louder as he blurts out to Job's three friends the unbelievable mighty works of God. God not only created the universe but He also controls the universe with His *unlimited power*.

Plant Spiritual Seeds

1. "Behold, God is exalted in his power [He is all-powerful]; who is a teacher like him?" (Job 36:22).
2. "God thunders wondrously with his voice [thunder is the voice of God]; he does great things that we cannot comprehend" (Job 37:5). Our five-year-old granddaughter announced during a thunderstorm, "Don't worry about the thunder; it is just God talking to us."
3. "For to the snow he says, 'Fall on the earth,' likewise to the downpour [rain], his mighty downpour" (Job 37:6). The Flood during the days of Noah was under God's control.

Elihu convinced Job and his friends that God is not only in control of nature, He also works miracles in people's lives.

God allowed Job to go through horrendous struggles in order to teach him, his friends, and us to trust God in all situations. My husband still thanks the Lord for protecting him through a spinout in the Big Ben Open Road Race. He breathed a sigh of relief and thanked the Lord when he could see the road. A car had spun out in front of him, creating a dust storm.

May each of us trust our Heavenly Father daily. Don't panic—pray.

Trust God Unconditionally

Lesson 6: Job 42

God does not always choose to calm a storm, but He could. We need to learn, as did Job, that regardless of our storms, God is at the helm and can change the course of any storm at any time. But first, we must unconditionally trust Him.

Job repented for not trusting God in his dire situations and said, "I had heard of you by the hearing of the ear, but now my eyes see you; therefore I despise myself, and *repent* in dust and ashes" (Job 42:5–6).

Because of Job's genuine repentance, "The Lord blessed the latter days of Job more than his beginning" (Job 42:12). God doubled the number of his sheep, camels, oxen, and donkeys, and blessed him with seven sons and three beautiful daughters.

After this, Job lived 140 years, seeing his children and their children to the fourth generation and dying old and full of years.

Plant Spiritual Seeds
1. Trust God, knowing He *can* subdue any storm in nature, in a nation, or in a person's life.
2. Trust God unconditionally, and be quick to repent when your faith fails.

The Lord Is My Shepherd
Psalm 23 KJV

The LORD is my shepherd; I shall not want.

He maketh me to lie down in green pastures: he leadeth me beside the still waters.

He restoreth my soul: he leadeth me in the paths of righteousness for his name's sake.

Yea, though I walk through the valley of the shadow of death, I will fear no evil: for thou art with me; thy rod and thy staff they comfort me.

Thou preparest a table before me in the presence of mine enemies: thou anointest my head with oil; my cup runneth over.

Surely goodness and mercy shall follow me all the days of my life: and I will dwell in the house of the Lord for ever.

Psalms

The book of Psalms covers many areas that affect our lives, from anger and fear to love and trust. Highlight verses that address your children's needs, and encourage Scripture memorization (offer monetary rewards).

Use the verses by:
- Praying them over your children
- Quoting them to your children

With 150 chapters, Psalms is the longest book in the Bible, so the alphabetized topics below are but a mere sampling of the book. As you read these verses, internalize their meanings and determine how you might plant them in your children's hearts.

When children learn what constitutes appropriate behavior, they will become more godly, obedient, and pleasant children.

Parenting Scriptures in Psalms

Anger
1. "Refrain from anger, and forsake wrath! Fret not yourself; it tends only to evil" (Ps. 37:8).
   - Do not let anger cause you to sin.
   - When anger rises within, pause and respond with kindness.
2. "The LORD is gracious and merciful, slow to anger and abounding in steadfast love" (Ps. 145:8).
   - Emulate God, and be *slow* to get angry. Practice *patience* and *compassion*, and be *rich in love toward others*.

Anxiety

"When the cares of my heart are many, your consolations cheer my soul" (Ps. 94:19).
   - If your heart is heavy, seek God's presence by listening to praise songs and hymns.
   - When anxiety creeps up on you, go outside and enjoy God's beautiful world.
   - Say no to stress.

Blessings
1. "Blessed are those who keep his testimonies [laws], who seek him with their whole heart, who also do no wrong, but walk in his ways!" (Ps. 119:2–3).
   - Blessed are those who never tire of obeying His Word and doing what is right.

2. "Blessed is the one who considers the poor! In the day of trouble the LORD delivers him" (Ps. 41:1).
   - Blessed are those who show kindness to the poor and needy. God blesses those who serve others.

Borrowing and Giving

"The wicked borrows but does not pay back, but the righteous is generous and gives" (Ps. 37:21).
- Set an example of generosity, and faithfully return borrowed items in perfect condition.

Cares

1. "Cast your burden on the LORD, and he will sustain you; he will *never permit* the righteous to be moved" (emphasis added) (Ps. 55:22).
   - When we stand firmly committed to God, He is there for us.
2. "For he is our God, and we are the people of his pasture, and the sheep of his hand" (95:7).
   - God can and will take care of us as a shepherd cares for his sheep.

Creation/Creator

1. "The earth is the LORD's and the fullness thereof, the world and those who dwell therein, for he has founded it upon the seas and established it upon the rivers" (Ps. 24:1–2).
   - God did a magnificent job when He created our beautiful world. Read the story of creation to your younger children, and encourage older children to learn about creation by reading Genesis 1.
2. "For you formed my inward parts; you knitted me together in my mother's womb" (Ps. 139:13).
   - Teach your children that God created them and knew them even before they were born.

Fear (Godly)

"Let all the earth fear the LORD; let all the inhabitants of the world stand in awe of him!" (Ps. 33:8).

- Everyone needs a healthy fear of the Lord, not to be afraid of Him but to the extent that they want to obey His commandments.
- Obedient children should also have a healthy fear of their parents.

Fear (Physical)

"When I am afraid, I put my trust in you" (Ps. 56:3).
- Seek God's help when fear crosses your path.
- One night, our granddaughter was fearful. I told her to pray, "I trust the Lord." Upon leaving her room, I could hear her repeating, "I trust the Lord, I trust the Lord."

Healing

"O Lord my God, I cried to you for help, and you have healed me" (Ps. 30:2).
- Pray for physical healing, but be willing to accept His will for your life.

Heaven

"One thing have I asked of the Lord, that will I seek after: that I may dwell in the house of the Lord all the days of my life, to gaze upon the beauty of the Lord and to inquire [pray] in his temple" (Ps. 27:4).
- Invite Jesus to live in your heart, and enjoy the assurance of an eternal life in Heaven with Him.

Love

1. "Your steadfast love, O Lord, extends to the heavens, your faithfulness to the clouds" (Ps. 36:5).
   - God's love is so great; it is higher than the heavens. That is a lot of love! This verse reminds me of the children's book *Guess How Much I Love You* by Sam McBratney. Check out this book from your library, and read it with your children.
   - God's love far surpasses parental love.
2. "But the steadfast love of the Lord is from everlasting to everlasting on those who fear him, and his righteousness to

children's children, to those who keep his covenant and remember to do his commandments" (emphasis added) (Ps. 103:17–18).
- Generations come, and generations go, but God's love is eternally with those who honor Him and keep His commandments.
- If you want your children to live godly lives, exemplify godly living before them.

Memorization

Memorization is much easier for those who are young. Start encouraging memorization at a young age, and *offer a reward for every verse memorized.*

Suggested verses to memorize:
- The Ten Commandments – Exodus 20:11–17
- King David's poem, "The Lord Is My Shepherd" – Psalm 23:1–6
- The Lord's Prayer – Matthew 6:9–13 (add "for Thine is the kingdom and the power and the glory forever. Amen.")
- The Sermon on the Mount – Matthew 5–7. Encourage children to read the Sermon on the Mount regularly, highlighting verses that speak to them and choosing those to memorize.

Omnipresent

1. "The angel of the LORD encamps around those who fear him, and he delivers them" (Ps. 34:7 NIV).
   - Pray and seek the protection of your guardian angel.
2. "Yet, I am always with you; you hold me by my right hand. You guide me with your counsel, and afterward you will take me into glory" (Ps. 73:23–24 NIV).
   - Daily reach out for the hand of God to guide you until He calls you home to Heaven.
   - Pray that your children and grandchildren will hold onto God's hand as well.
3. "O LORD, you have searched me and known me! You know when I sit down and when I rise up; you discern my thoughts from afar. You search out my path and my lying down and

are acquainted with all my ways. Even *before* a word is on my tongue, behold, O LORD, you know it altogether" (emphasis added) (Ps. 139:1–4).
- God knows us better than we know ourselves. Seek His guidance.

4. "As the mountains surround Jerusalem, so the LORD surrounds his people, both now and forevermore" (Ps. 125:2 NIV).
    - The Lord is omnipresent with you and your family. Acknowledge His presence, and seek His protection.

Path

1. "I will instruct you and teach you in the way you should go; I will counsel you with my eye upon you" (Ps. 32:8).
    - God is our teacher and counselor. Listen to Him.
2. "Your word is a lamp for my feet, and a light on my path" (Ps. 119:105 NIV).
    - May the Light of the World show us the way.

Peace

"How good and pleasant it is when God's people live together in unity!" (Ps. 133:1 NIV).
- Make it your goal to live in peace and unity with everyone.

Praise

"My mouth is filled with your praise, and with your glory all the day" (Ps. 71:8).
- Praise God continually.
- Live a Spirit-controlled life.

Prayer

1. "Give ear, O LORD, to my prayer; listen to my plea for grace. In the day of my trouble I call upon you, for you answer me" (Ps. 86:6–7).
    - Pray to God for mercy and help. He will always hear and answer your prayers. Sometimes, He says yes, and other times He says no or wait.

2. "The Lord is in his holy temple; the Lord is on his heavenly throne" (Ps. 11:4 NIV).
   - When you pray, remember that you are praying to the Creator of the universe who rules the world from His holy temple.
   - Sing the song "The Lord Is in His Holy Temple" before you pray. As you sing, picture God seated on His throne, ready to hear your prayers.

Protection
1. "Keep me safe, my God, for in you I take refuge" (Ps. 16:1 NIV).
   - May Your indwelling Spirit protect me!
2. "O God, be not far from me; O my God, make haste to help me!" (Ps. 71:12).
   - God is always near, awaiting your call for help.

Rejoice
"This is the day that the Lord has made; let us rejoice and be glad in it" (Ps. 118:24).
   - As your children leave for school, remind them that this is the day the Lord has made and to rejoice and be happy. Nurture your children to have *internal and external joy*. Joy is a wonderful gift.
   - When selecting gifts, choose gifts that bring *joy*.

Righteousness (Right Standing with God)
The righteous flourish like the palm tree
    and grow like a cedar in Lebanon.
They are planted in the house of the Lord;
    they flourish in the courts of our God.
They still bear fruit in old age;
    they are ever full of sap and green,
to declare that the Lord is upright;
    he is my rock, and there is *no unrighteousness in him* (emphasis added).

—Ps. 92:12–15

- A personal relationship with the Lord changes your life profoundly.
- Seek to live a God-fearing life, and bond with your Heavenly Father.

Seeking

"My heart says of you, 'Seek his face!' Your face, LORD, I will seek" (Ps. 27:8 NIV).
- Write this Scripture in the front of your Bible, and daily seek Him by reading His Word.

Sin

"Have mercy on me, O God, according to your unfailing love; according to your great compassion blot out my transgressions. Wash away all my iniquity and cleanse me from my sin" (Ps. 51:1–2 NIV).
- Like King David, seek God's forgiveness whenever you sin (reread Psalm 51).

Tongue

"Keep your tongue from evil and your lips from telling lies. Turn from evil and do good; seek peace and pursue it" (Ps. 34:13–14 NIV).

1. *Think* before you speak.

    T—is it *true?*
    H—is it *helpful?*
    I—is it *inspiring?*
    N—is it *necessary?*
    K—is it *kind?*

2. "My tongue is the pen of a skillful writer" (Ps. 45:1 NIV).
    - A skilled writer carefully chooses the words he or she writes. Likewise, we should carefully choose the words we speak.

3. "Set a guard, O LORD, over my mouth; keep watch over the door of my lips!" (Ps. 141:3).
    - Pray this prayer daily over your children and yourself. Have your children picture the Lord standing in front of their lips, ready to *filter* their speech.

Trust

"I hate those who pay regard to worthless idols, but I trust in the LORD" (Ps. 31:6).

- *Trust in the Lord*, not idols. Idols are anything or anyone that we prioritize over our Heavenly Father. Idols cannot answer prayers.

Victory

"For not in my bow do I trust, nor can my sword save me. But you have saved us from our foes and have put to shame those who hate us" (Ps. 44:6–7).

- God enjoys meeting the needs of His children. Seek His help, and praise Him when help arrives. God helped Gideon's small army of 300 men root out the Midianites who had terrorized Judah for years. Gideon gave God credit for the victory.
- Remember, obedience brings success.

Word of God

1. "The words of the LORD are pure words, like silver refined in a furnace on the ground, purified seven times" (Ps. 12:6).
   - God's Word is infallible—it has no mistakes.
2. "The law of their God is in their hearts; their feet do not slip" (Ps. 37:31 NIV).
   - The secret to living righteously (in right standing with God) is to know and obey His Word. Through memorizing and reading His Word, we put God's laws in our hearts.
3. "I delight to do your will, O my God; your law is within my heart" (Ps. 40:8).
   - Plant God's Word in your children's hearts, and watch them walk uprightly.

Words

"May these words of my mouth and this meditation of my heart be pleasing in your sight, LORD, my Rock and my Redeemer" (Ps. 19:14 NIV).

- Have your children memorize this verse. Encourage all children to *pray this verse* before they speak or before they give an oral presentation.

Proverbs and Ecclesiastes

It seems only rational that King Solomon would be the author of Proverbs and Ecclesiastes. Why? Because his father, King David, had grown in wisdom through a life of hard knocks and had passed that wisdom down to him. It would also be because God, through a dream, gave Solomon an opportunity to ask Him for anything, and he chose wisdom to better rule Israel. God responded and gave him *immeasurable* wisdom. Read Proverbs, and improve your parenting skills.

There are 31 chapters in Proverbs—one chapter for each day of the month. If we were to read a chapter a day, month after month, we would indeed become wiser people. As it is wise to associate with those who are more knowledgeable than you or I, it is also wise to read what wiser people have written.

There are six parenting lessons in the first 10 chapters of Proverbs, and following those lessons is an alphabetized list of parenting proverbs. *Highlight the proverbs* that would benefit your children, and select proverbs to memorize.

Wisdom Should Flow through Us to Our Children

Lesson 1: Proverbs 1, 4

May Solomon's godly wisdom flow through us to our children. May we become better parents.

1. "Hear, my son, your father's instruction, and forsake not your mother's teaching" (Prov. 1:8).
   - Teach children to honor and respect their parents.
   - Teach children to listen closely to you and honor you.
2. "My son, be attentive to my words; incline your ear to my sayings. Let them not escape from your sight; keep them within your heart. For they are life to those who find them, and healing to all their flesh" (Prov. 4:20–22).
   - Plan a Scripture memorization program with your family. Collect memory verses in a sack. Memorizing God's Word empowers a family to become healthier *spiritually* as well as *physically*. "I pray that all may go well with you and that you may be in good health, as it goes well with your soul" (3 John 2).
3. "Put away from you crooked speech, and put devious talk [lies] far from you" (Prov. 4:24).
   - Solomon reminded the next generation to please their Heavenly Father with their *speech* and to *never lie*.

4. Stay on the straight and narrow path: "Do not swerve to the right or to the left; turn your foot away from evil" (Prov. 4:27).
   - May your family walk on the straight and narrow pathway that leads to Heaven.

Plant Spiritual Seeds

1. Never forget that you are God's ambassadors to *all* children—to those in your home, your neighborhood, your community, your nation, and the world.
2. Wisely exemplify godly behavior before your children, and watch them follow your walk with the Lord.
3. May your children, as adults, exemplify godly wisdom and create generational blessings.

Flee Sexual Immorality

Lesson 2: Proverbs 5

The proverbs here emphasize the importance of fleeing sexual temptations. Share with your sons the two tenets of wisdom that encourage men to stay faithful to their wives and away from adulterous women.

1. Flee sexual immorality: "Now then, my sons, listen to me; do not turn aside from what I say. Keep to a path far from her, do not go near the door of her house" (Prov. 5:7–8 NIV).
   - Listen to *God's advice*. If a girl or woman looks enticing, have self-discipline, and do not go near the door of her house.
2. Stay faithful to your spouse: "Drink water from your own cistern, flowing water from your own well" (Prov. 5:15).
   - Love and be loved by your own spouse.

After King David sinned sexually, he repented and acknowledged he had made a grave mistake. Read David's prayer of repentance from Psalm 51 (see pages 104–105).

Plant Spiritual Seeds

1. Teach your children the seventh commandment: "You shall not commit adultery" (Exod. 20:14).
2. May each of your children walk a godly path, fleeing even a hint of sexual immorality.

3. Work diligently on being faithful in your marriage. Proverbs 5:15 reminds us to enjoy water from our own cistern (your spouse). Parents, good examples are imperative.
4. Remember, the sins of the father or mother pass through the family to the third and fourth generations. Choose to deactivate all generational curses, especially sexual ones.

Don't Be Lazy

Lesson 3: Proverbs 6, 10

An ant bed provides a teaching moment with your children or grandchildren.

> *Go to the ant, O sluggard;*
> *consider her ways, and be wise.*
> *Without having any chief,*
> *officer, or ruler,*
> *she prepares her bread in summer*
> *and gathers her food in harvest.*
> *How long will you lie there, O sluggard?*
> *When will you arise from your sleep?*
> *A little sleep, a little slumber,*
> *a little folding of the hands to rest,*
> *and poverty will come upon you like a robber,*
> *and want like an armed man.*
>
> —Prov. 6:6–11

With your children, point out that ants stay focused and work diligently throughout the day. Whenever you have a job to do, remember to stay focused, and never stop until the job is completed.

"Lazy hands make for poverty, but diligent hands bring wealth" (Prov. 10:4 NIV). Talk about and instill a hardworking mentality in the hearts and minds of your children.

My dad always said, "Time to get up and going; the early bird gets the worm." I still sense the need to get up and be productive.

Plant Spiritual Seeds
1. Work like an ant, and enjoy success.
2. Be productive: "The early bird gets the worm."
3. Work diligently as unto the Lord.

Seven Traits God Detests

Lesson 4: Proverbs 6, 10

In Proverbs 6:16–19, King Solomon listed seven traits that God detests.

Sing with your children "Oh Be Careful," and with each stanza, shout out one of the detestable traits.

"Oh Be Careful"

- Trait 1: Haughty Eyes
  "O be careful little eyes what you see, *no haughtiness*!
  O be careful little eyes what you see, *no haughtiness*!
  For the Father up above
  Is looking down with love,
  So be careful little eyes what you see, *no haughtiness*!"

****

- Trait 2: A Lying Tongue
  "O be careful little tongue what you say, *never lie*!"
  etc.

****

- Trait 3: Hands That Shed Innocent Blood
  "O be careful little hands what you do, *be kind*!"
  etc.

- Trait 4: A Heart That Devises Wicked Schemes
  "O be careful little minds what you think, *no evil plans!*"
  etc.

****

- Trait 5: Feet That Are Quick to Rush to Evil
  "O be careful little feet where you go, *flee evil!*"
  etc.

****

- Trait 6: A False Witness Who Pours Out Lies
  "O be careful little tongue when you speak, *tell the truth!*"
  etc.

****

- Trait 7: A Person Who Stirs Up Dissension
  "O be careful little heart, be full of love, *love others!*"
  etc.
  Each trait constitutes a detestable sin to avoid.

****

Bible Stories to Help Children Avoid "Committing a Detestable Sin"

1: Haughty Eyes
David's army, "Haughtiness Is a Sin" (page 106); women's appearances, "Refrain from Haughtiness" (page 195).

2: A Lying Tongue
Joseph's brothers told their dad that a wild animal had killed Joseph, "Be a Role Model – Like Joseph" (page 15).

3: Hands That Shed Innocent Blood
David had Uriah killed, "Confess and Seek Forgiveness for Your Sins" (page 104); David refused to kill Saul, "Choose to Return Evil with Kindness" (page 97).

4: A Heart That Devises Wicked Schemes

Joseph's brothers sold him to an Egyptian caravan, "Be Role Model – Like Joseph" (page 15).

5: Feet That Are Quick to Rush into Evil

Achan steals items during the Jericho battle for personal gain, "Obedience Brings Success; Disobedience Brings Consequences" (page 68).

6: A False Witness Who Pours Out Lies

Gehazi lied to Elisha to cover up his evil act, "Gehazi's Consequence for Lying: Leprosy" (page 116).

7: A Person Who Stirs Up Dissension

Rebekah, the mother of Esau and Jacob, created dissension between her two sons, "Never Rejoice over Others' Misfortunes" (page 258).

Plant Spiritual Seeds

During drive time, sing "O Be Careful" with your children, and shout out the seven detestable things (sins). (You can look up the melody to this song on YouTube.)

Transform Foolish Children into Wise Children

Lesson 5: Proverbs 10

Children are born foolish, but with parental guidance, they can develop wisdom (knowing and doing what is right). Wise children bring joy and peace to parents and to their Heavenly Father.

- "A *wise* son makes a glad father, but a *foolish* son is a sorrow to his mother" (emphasis added) (Prov. 10:1).
- "He who gathers crops in summer is a prudent son, but he who sleeps during harvest is a disgraceful son" (Prov. 10:5 NIV).
- "Whoever walks in *integrity* walks securely, but he who makes his ways *crooked* will be found out" (emphasis added) (Prov. 10:9).
- "Whoever *heeds* discipline shows the way to life, but whoever ignores correction leads others astray" (emphasis added) (Prov. 10:17 NIV).
- "The lips of the *righteous* know what is acceptable, but the mouth of the *wicked*, what is perverse" (emphasis added) (Prov. 10:32).

Children usually emulate their parents' walks, so parents, be careful how you live. Make wise choices.

Plant Spiritual Seeds
1. Teach your children to be wise, knowing right from wrong.
2. The more Scripture a child understands, the wiser he or she becomes. Choose memory verses that develop wisdom.
3. Sing the song "The Wise Man Built His House" (available on the Internet), which teaches that a home, grounded on the Word of God, stands firm.

Address Life's Issues with a Proverb

Lesson 6: Proverbs 11–31; Ecclesiastes 1–12

Solomon reminded his readers to "incline your ear, and hear the words of the wise, and apply your heart to my knowledge, for it will be pleasant if you keep them within you, if all of them are ready on your lips" (Prov. 22:17–18).

Below is an alphabetized list of proverbs our Heavenly Father inspired Solomon to write. As you read these proverbs, highlight the ones that would help your children develop wisdom, and together select proverbs to memorize. Write the proverbs you want to memorize on index cards, and place them in a memory sack. After memorizing a verse, drop it into another sack labeled Review Sack, and review those verses regularly.

Remember, rewards encourage memorization.

Anger

1. "Good sense makes one slow to anger, and it is his glory to overlook an offense" (Prov. 19:11).
    - Be slow to become angry, and overlook when others wrong you.
2. "A fool gives full vent to his spirit, but a wise man *quietly* holds it [anger] back" (emphasis added) (Prov. 29:11).
    - Do not vent your anger. Instead of becoming angry, take some deep breaths.
3. "A man of wrath stirs up strife, and one given to anger causes much transgression [sin]" (Prov. 29:22).
    - Self-control protects you from sinning.

Discipline

The purpose of discipline is to teach children right from wrong. Since children are born with a sinful nature, we need to be proactive and train them to become pleasant, loving, and genuinely kind people. Plant as many spiritual seeds in the hearts and minds of your children as soon as possible, and never stop.

When children misbehave, sit down and encourage them to self-correct. Give them several opportunities to mend their ways before administering discipline. Some forms of discipline include spanking, time-outs, and taking away electronics, favorite toys, or TV time. Assigning a chore to be completed also works wonders. When our son was a teenager, we grounded him until he cleaned all our flowerbeds. It was a win-win situation—the flowerbeds looked great, and his behavior changed, which was our ultimate goal.

Choose an appropriate punishment for the age of your child and for the misbehavior.

1. "The rod and reproof give wisdom, but a child left to himself brings shame to his mother" (Prov. 29:15).
   - Do not miss an opportunity to discipline. Through discipline, your children learn right from wrong, which gives them wisdom to succeed in life.
2. "Train up a child in the way he should go; even when he is old he will not depart from it" (Prov. 22:6).
   - A disciplined child will develop integrity.

Drinking

1. "Wine is a mocker, strong drink a brawler, and whoever is led astray by it is not wise" (Prov. 20:1).
   - Alcohol can create problems.

Giving

1. "Whoever brings blessing will be enriched, and one who waters will himself be watered" (Prov. 11:25).
   - Those who plant blessings, reap blessings.
2. "*Honor* the LORD with your wealth and with the firstfruits of all your produce; then your *barns will be filled with plenty*, and your vats will be bursting with wine" (emphasis added) (Prov. 3:9–10).

- Tithe (10 percent) to the Lord even before paying your bills, and your barns will be full.

Good Name
1. "A good name is better than precious ointment [perfume], and the day of death than the day of birth" (Eccles. 7:1).
   - A good name is priceless. Maintain its luster, and avoid tarnishing it.
   - The day of your death is more precious than the day of your birth.

Good Person
1. "A good person leaves an inheritance for their children's children, but a sinner's wealth is stored up for the righteous" (Prov. 13:22 NIV).
   - Do not just plan for today; plan for future generations as well.

Gossip
1. "Whoever goes about slandering reveals secrets, but he who is trustworthy in spirit keeps a thing covered" (Prov. 11:13).
   - Keep secrets, and become known as a trustworthy person.
2. "For lack of wood the fire goes out, and where there is no whisperer, quarreling ceases" (Prov. 26:20).
   - Use self-control, and remain silent in order to silence gossip.

Healing
1. "My son, pay attention to what I say; turn your ear to my words. Do not let them out of your sight, keep them within your heart; for they are life to those who find them and health to one's whole body" (Prov. 4:20–22 NIV).
   - Living out the Word of God in your life brings you good health.
2. "Be not wise in your own eyes; fear the LORD, and turn away from evil. It will be *healing to your flesh* and *refreshment* to your bones" (emphasis added) (Prov. 3:7–8).
   - The Word is like medicine to the body.

Heart

1. "The heart of the wise makes his speech judicious and adds persuasiveness to his lips" (Prov. 16:23).
   - The words of a wise person are worth heeding.
2. "A joyful heart is good medicine, but a crushed spirit dries up the bones" (Prov. 17:22).
   - Share jokes with family and friends, and enjoy a daily dose of medicine—laughter!

Path for Life

1. "Whoever walks with the wise becomes wise, but the companion of fools will suffer harm" (Prov. 13:20).
   - Friends affect your life. Be wise, and choose friends who know and do what is right.
2. "Every way of a man is right in his own eyes, but the Lord weighs the heart" (Prov. 21:2).
   - May your heart always be in tune with His.

Peace

1. "Hatred stirs up strife, but love covers all offenses" (Prov. 10:12).
   - Love covers a multitude of sins.
2. "The vexation [annoyance] of a fool is known at once, but the prudent ignores an insult" (Prov. 12:16).
   - Never respond too quickly to a troubled person; instead, pause, smile, and pray for them.
3. "If anyone returns evil for good, evil will not depart from his house" (Prov. 17:13).
   - Always reciprocate kindness with kindness, never evil for kindness as Nabal did when he refused to feed David and his men after they had protected his herd from raiders.

Punishment of the Wicked

1. "Be assured, an evil person will not go unpunished, but the offspring of the righteous will be delivered" (Prov. 11:21).
   - Live righteously to ensure your children will inherit generational blessings instead of generational curses.

Praise
1. "Let someone else praise you, and not your own mouth; an outsider, and not your own lips" (Prov. 27:2 NIV).
   - Pat others, not yourself, on the back. Be humble, not prideful.

Return Evil with Kindness
1. "If your *enemy* is hungry, give him food to eat; if he is thirsty, give him water to drink. In doing this, you will heap burning coals on his head, and the LORD will reward you" (emphasis added) (Prov. 25:21–22 NIV).
   - God *commands* us to show kindness to our enemies.

Righteousness (Right Standing with God)
1. "If the righteous is repaid on earth, how much more the wicked and the sinner!" (Prov. 11:31).
   - All people reap what they sow on this earth, be it good or bad.
2. "Surely there is *not* a righteous man on earth who does good and *never sins*" (emphasis added) (Eccles. 7:20).
   - *All have sinned and fallen short of righteousness.* This is the reason we look to Jesus to forgive our sins.

Sin and Forgiveness
1. "Whoever conceals his transgressions will not prosper, but he who confesses and forsakes them will obtain mercy" (Prov. 28:13).
   - Mercy and prosperity are for those who confess their sins and determine never to repeat those sins again.

Speech
1. "A soft answer turns away wrath, but a harsh word stirs up anger" (Prov. 15:1).
   - Answer with kind words; do not stir up anger.
2. "Whoever keeps his mouth and his tongue keeps himself out of trouble" (Prov. 21:23).
3. "Let every person be quick to hear, slow to speak, slow to anger" (James 1:19).
4. "Do not let your mouth lead you into sin" (Eccles. 5:6 NIV).
   - "On the day of judgment people will give account for every careless word they speak" (Matt. 12:36).

Trust

1. "Trust in the LORD with all your heart, and do not lean on your own understanding. In all your ways acknowledge him, and he will *make straight your paths*" (emphasis added) (Prov. 3:5–6).
   - Trust in the Lord with all your heart, and you will not veer off His path for your life.

Vows to God

1. "When you vow a vow to God, do not delay paying it, for he has no pleasure in fools. Pay what you vow. It is better that you should not vow than that you should vow and not pay" (Eccles. 5:4–5).
   - Fulfill all your vows to God and people.

Wisdom

1. "The father of a righteous child has great joy; a man who fathers a wise son rejoices in him" (Prov. 23:24 NIV).
   - To reap a godly son or daughter, sow godly seeds.
   - A righteous (wise) son or daughter brings happiness, joy, and peace.
   - It serves a man well to know and do what is right.

Work

1. "The LORD detests dishonest scales, but accurate weights find favor with him" (Prov. 11:1 NIV).
   - Be wise; have integrity. "For the eyes of the Lord are on the righteous, and his ears are open to their prayer. But the face of the Lord is against those who do evil" (1 Pet. 3:12).
   - Be wise in how you earn as well as how you spend your money.
2. "Love not sleep, lest you come to poverty; open your eyes, and you will have plenty of bread" (Prov. 20:13).
   - Get a *good* night's sleep, work hard, and enjoy success.
3. "Through laziness, the rafters sag; because of idle hands, the house leaks" (Eccles. 10:18 NIV).
   - Dads and moms, be industrious. Your children are watching you. Remember, "The early bird gets the worm."

✳✳✳✳✳✳✳✳✳✳✳✳✳✳✳✳✳

Final Thoughts from Solomon

"The end of the matter; all has been heard. *Fear God and keep his commandments, for this is the whole duty of man.* For God will bring every deed into judgment, with every secret thing, whether good or evil" (emphasis added) (Eccles. 12:13–14).

We will *all* be judged for the lives we have lived.

Final Thoughts from Solomon.

Isaiah

Isaiah is one of the most important books in the Bible because of the many prophecies verifying that Jesus was and is the Son of God. It is mind-boggling to think these verses prophesied the birth of God's Son, Jesus, 400 years *before* His birth. Isaiah focuses on the fact that through the Messiah, we have salvation.

Here are some of Isaiah's prophecies:

- The Messiah (Jesus) would be born to a virgin (Isa. 7:14).
- The Messiah (Jesus) would be an heir of King David (Isa. 9:7).
- There would be a voice of one (John the Baptist) in the wilderness, crying out to prepare the way for the Messiah's (Jesus's) ministry (Isa. 40:3–5).
- The Messiah (Jesus) would be spat upon and beaten prior to crucifixion (Isa. 50:6).
- The Messiah's (Jesus's) shed blood would atone for our sins (Isa. 53:5).
- The Messiah (Jesus) would be buried in a rich man's tomb (Isa. 53:9).

Isaiah's teachings provide us with 12 parenting lessons.

Stop Doing Wrong; Learn to Do Right

Lesson 1: Isaiah 1

Judah had decayed to the extent that serious consequences were on the horizon. Even after experiencing discipline, they were still sinful, ignoring God and worshiping idols.

But God showed compassion and mercy by giving Judah another opportunity to repent: "Remove the evil of your deeds from before my eyes; cease to do evil, learn to do good . . . though your sins are like scarlet, they shall be as white as snow; though they are red like crimson, they shall become like wool" (Isa. 1:16–18).

It pleases our Heavenly Father when we exemplify godly behavior, and as we raise well-behaved, obedient children who live according to the Word of God, we give peace and joy to our Heavenly Father and to ourselves.

Plant Spiritual Seeds

1. Countries and individuals alike need to stop doing wrong and learn to do right. Everyone needs a mindset to go and sin no more.
2. Parents, nip rebellion in the bud with discipline.
3. As parents, have a game plan for training your children to obey and walk in the ways of the Lord.

Refrain from Haughtiness

Lesson 2: Isaiah 3

As mentioned earlier, Solomon taught that haughtiness was one of the seven things (sins) that God detests. At this point in Judah's history, haughtiness had become a major problem.

> The LORD said:
> Because the daughters of Zion are haughty
>   and walk with outstretched necks,
>   glancing wantonly with their eyes,
> mincing along as they go,
>   tinkling with their feet,
> therefore the Lord will strike with a scab
>   the heads of the daughters of Zion,
>   and the LORD will lay bare their secret parts.
> —Isa. 3:16–17

The women sought attention by their outward appearances and their walks. They had forgotten that true beauty was internal. Everyone, parents and children alike, needs to bring glory to God and avoid haughtiness. Dress in such a way that when people look at you, they see your face, not your attire. Your face is the outer reflection of your inner self. Proverbs 27:19 says it so well: "As in water face reflects face, so the heart of man reflects the man."

Mothers, encourage your daughters to dress modestly. It will draw attention to their faces and reflect their inner beauty.

Plant Spiritual Seeds
1. Live a life that pleases God. May His presence in your heart be evident to all.
2. Look in a mirror and ask yourself, "Do I bring glory to God?"
3. If you become haughty, repent, seek forgiveness, and evaluate your *walk* and *dress*.
4. Sing "Oh Be Careful" and shout out *"no haughtiness"* (see page 180).

Draw Near to Him

Lesson 3: Isaiah 6

In Chapter 6, Isaiah had a beautiful vision of the Lord in His temple.

> *In the year that King Uzziah died I saw the Lord sitting upon a throne, high and lifted up; and the train of his robe filled the temple. Above him stood the seraphim. Each had six wings: with two he covered his face, and with two he covered his feet, and with two he flew. And one called to another and said: "Holy, holy, holy is the* Lord *of hosts; the whole earth is full of his glory!" And the foundations of the thresholds shook at the voice of him who called, and the house was filled with smoke.*
>
> —Isa. 6:1–4

It is obvious that this Scripture inspired Edwin O. Excell to write the song "The Lord Is in His Holy Temple." If you are unfamiliar with this song, find it on the Internet. Before you pray, draw near to God by closing your eyes and singing this song. Picture your Heavenly Father seated on His throne with His train filling the temple, ready to hear your prayers. Then pray with the assurance that your Heavenly Father is listening.

Plant Spiritual Seeds

1. "The Lord Is in His Holy Temple" (song available on the Internet):

    "The Lord is in His holy temple (repeat); let all the earth keep silence (repeat). Before Him keep silence, keep silence before Him."

2. Sing "The Lord Is in His Holy Temple" with your children before their nighttime prayers. This song draws them into the presence of the King of kings and the Creator of the universe.

3. Know that the Lord of lords resides not only in His holy temple but also in our hearts.

Stand Firm in Your Faith Like King Ahaz

Lesson 4: Isaiah 7

When King Ahaz of Judah became *fearful* that Aram (Syria) and Ephraim (Israel) would overtake Judah, God spoke to him through Isaiah: "If you are not firm in faith, you will not be firm at all" (Isa. 7:9).

Isaiah told King Ahaz to ask the Lord for a sign that Judah would not fall if he stood firm in his faith. But Ahaz replied, "I will not ask, I will not put the Lord to the test" (Isa. 7:12). Then Isaiah said, "Hear then, O house of David! Is it too little for you to weary men, that you weary my God also? Therefore the Lord himself will give you a sign. Behold, *the virgin shall conceive and bear a son, and shall call his name Immanuel* [God with us]" (emphasis added) (Isa. 7:13–14). This prophecy of Jesus is renowned.

Even though Ahaz would not ask for a sign, he still heeded Isaiah's words and stood firm in his faith. Therefore, Judah *withstood* the invasion of Aram (Syria) and Ephraim (Israel). Our children today need to stand firm in their faith as well. Everyone needs to stand firm.

A quarterback on our local high school football team exemplified the meaning of "standing firm" for the Lord. One day, a friend overheard a conversation among some high school girls who were waiting to be seated in a restaurant. One young girl announced that she was going to ask the quarterback out. Her friends replied, "He would not go out with you." She said she would wait until after football season. Her friends still responded, "No, he will not go out with you; you're not his type."

This young man's reputation of standing firm in his faith was well established. These girls were correct when they insisted that he would not go out with her. He was a great role model for his teammates, his classmates, his community, and his Lord.

One person can make a big difference. Be that person!

Plant Spiritual Seeds

1. Stand firm for the Lord, and let your light shine for Him every day, all day.
2. When your children stand firm in their faith, their reputations bring glory to their Heavenly Father.

Bond with Your Heavenly Father
Lesson 5: Isaiah 29

In Chapter 29, Isaiah revealed a serious problem. "And the Lord said: 'Because this people draw near with their mouth and honor me with their lips, while their *hearts* are far from me'" (emphasis added) (Isa. 29:13). The Judeans had head knowledge of their Heavenly Father, but their hearts were out of sync with His. They knew the Word but failed to embrace it.

At the young age of five, our son taught me a lesson. I asked him, "Who is your best friend?" He said without hesitation, "I don't want to hurt your feelings, Mom, but Jesus is my best friend." His response truly amazed me. Starting as a toddler, he had gone weekly with me to teach flannel-board Bible lessons, and by his answer, I realized that spiritually, he was far beyond his years. Through the many Bible stories, songs, and prayers, he had drawn near to his Heavenly Father. That day, I learned that children are never too young to develop a heartfelt relationship with God.

Spending time with family and friends strengthens the bond between family and friends. The same is true with our Heavenly Father. When we spend time reading our Bibles and devotional books, praying, or just listening to Christian music, we are strengthening the bond with our Heavenly Father. This bonding gives us a heartfelt love for Him with a desire to serve Him. Likewise, when we bond with family and friends, we love them and want to help them.

Plant Spiritual Seeds
1. Bond with your Heavenly Father and your earthly friends.
2. May each of your children develop a heartfelt relationship with their Heavenly Father and seek to serve Him.

The Messiah Came as a Good Shepherd, with Power and Might

Lesson 6: Isaiah 40

Isaiah prophesied that the Messiah would come with power and might and would be a good shepherd to His flock:

> *Behold, the Lord God comes with might,*
> *   and his arm rules for him;*
> *behold, his reward is with him. . . .*
> *He will tend his flock like a shepherd;*
> *   he will gather the lambs in his arms;*
> *he will carry them in his bosom,*
> *   and gently lead those that are with young.*
>
> —Isa. 40:10–11

His power and might became evident to all when Jesus Christ calmed storms, healed *all* who were sick, and freed those who were demon possessed. Just as we do not receive electrical power until we plug into electricity, our Heavenly Father cannot help us until we connect with Him. He is all-powerful, but first we must pray and seek His help.

As a Good Shepherd, Jesus tends to His flock and meets the needs of His sheep.

Jesus fulfills both of these prophecies proclaimed by Isaiah.

Our daughter and son-in-law chose "Savior Like a Shepherd Lead Us" to be sung at their wedding. How appropriate! Every couple needs the strength and guidance of the Good Shepherd as they live their lives, and especially as they raise their children.

Plant Spiritual Seeds

1. Know that the Good Shepherd (Jesus) can and will take care of your needs and help you as you raise your children.
2. Instead of being a single parent, seek the help of your Heavenly Father.
3. Remember, there is nothing too hard for God.

God Gives Strength to the Weary

Lesson 7: Isaiah 40

> He [God] gives power to the faint,
>   and to him who has no might he increases strength.
> Even youths shall faint and become weary,
>   and young men shall fall exhausted;
> but they who wait for the L<small>ORD</small> shall renew their strength;
>   they shall mount up with wings like eagles;
> they shall run and not be weary;
>   they shall walk and not faint.
>
> —Isa. 40:29–31

When weakness sets in, stop and remember that you have a Heavenly Father who can give you strength. Pray and seek His help.

Even though I used to have plenty of physical endurance, as time passes, there are days when this verse applies to me. I have weak days; you have weak days. We all have times when we need our strength renewed. Take time to draw near to Him and receive His strength, remembering that "my help *comes* from the L<small>ORD</small>, *the Maker* of heaven and earth" (emphasis added) (Ps. 121:2 NIV). Call on the Lord when you need help.

Betty and her husband Rudy took his 96-year-old aunt on a trip. Because his aunt had extreme muscle loss and was confined to a wheelchair, Betty was fearful that rest stops might become a challenge. Only time would tell. At the first rest stop, Betty prayed for angelic help, and as she reached down to lift Aunt Nancy up, surprisingly,

Nancy stood up on her own and moved over with ease. What joy Betty experienced when the Lord extended His helping hand. God is good.

Seek God's help in times of need.

Plant Spiritual Seeds

1. When you are weak, look upward and ask your Heavenly Father for strength—spiritual, physical, mental, or social.
2. Teach your children to pray for mental strength before and during tests.
3. Memorize these verses:
    - "I can do all things through him [Christ] who strengthens me" (Phil. 4:13). My mother sent this verse to me when I was overwrought with college exams.
    - "My help comes from the LORD, the Maker of heaven and earth" (Ps.121:2 NIV).
4. In an uncomfortable social situation, seek God's presence, let His light shine through you, and be an ambassador for Him.

Through Troubled Waters, God Is with Us

Lesson 8: Isaiah 43

Our Heavenly Father is present whenever we face trials and tribulations beyond our ability to handle. Here's what the Lord said:

> ***When*** *you pass through the waters, I will be with you;*
> *and through the rivers, they shall not overwhelm you;*
> ***when*** *you walk through fire you shall not be burned,*
> *and the flame shall not consume you.*
> *For I am the* L<small>ORD</small> *your God,*
> *the Holy One of Israel, your Savior. . . .*
> ***Fear not, for I am with you***" (emphasis added).
>
> —Isa. 43:2–3, 5

Note that verse 2 does not begin with *if* but *when*—it is inevitable that we will all pass through deep waters or face fiery situations. Set an example for your children by literally giving God your problems and letting Him guide you safely to the other side. Your children will one day have their own rivers to cross or fires to extinguish, and they will *remember the strong example you exhibited*.

Plant Spiritual Seeds

1. Do not fear or have anxiety when facing deep waters, flames, or tribulations. Instead, hold on tightly to your Heavenly Father's hand to get you through. Trust God, like Job!

2. Have a mindset to say no when tempted to sin in order to *avoid* deep waters and the flames of distress. Pray for those facing temptations today.
3. Relax, and let God be your life jacket or your fireproof suit. To avoid troubles, stay on the straight and narrow path.

God Can Blot Out Your Sins

Lesson 9: Isaiah 43–45

God makes it very clear that He forgives sins:

- "I, even I, am he who *blots out* your transgressions, for my own sake, and remembers your sins no more" (emphasis added) (Isa. 43:25 NIV).
- "I have *blotted out* your transgressions like a cloud and your sins like mist; return to me, for I have redeemed you" (emphasis added) (Isa. 44:22).
- "Turn to me and be saved, all the ends of the earth! For I am God, and there is no other" (Isa. 45:22).

What a blessing knowing that forgiveness is permanent—our sins are erased!

If God could bless King David with a clean slate, He can forgive anyone who seeks forgiveness (page 104).

Once forgiven, go and sin no more!

Plant Spiritual Seeds

1. God can give anyone a fresh start––first, however, that person needs to repent (go, and sin no more).
2. Know that when God grants you forgiveness, it is permanent, and He *never* remembers your sin.
3. There is a stipulation before you receive forgiveness––*you must forgive others*.

Memorize this verse: "Be kind to one another, tenderhearted, forgiving one another, as *God in Christ forgave you*" (emphasis added) (Eph. 4:32).

Receive Salvation and Eternal Life
Lesson 10: Isaiah 53, 55

Isaiah prophesied this:

> But he [Jesus] was pierced for our transgressions;
>   he was crushed for our iniquities;
> upon him was the chastisement that brought us peace,
>   and with his wounds we are healed.
> All we like sheep have gone astray;
>   we have turned—every one—to his own way;
> and the Lord has laid on him
>   the iniquity of us all.
>
> —Isa. 53:5–6

Isaiah gives the staples of a Christian *salvation experience*:

> Seek the Lord while he may be found;
>   call upon him while he is near;
> let the wicked forsake his way,
>   and the unrighteous man his thoughts;
> let him return to the Lord, that he may have compassion on him,
>   and to our God, for he will abundantly pardon.
>
> —Isa. 55:6–7

Give your children a strong, spiritual foundation with a yearning to know the Lord. Pray that each of your children responds to the Holy Spirit's invitation and invites Him into his or her heart. As they grow spiritually, the gifts of the Holy Spirit will be manifested in their lives: love, joy, peace, patience, kindness, goodness, faithfulness, gentleness, and self-control (Gal. 5:22).

Plant Spiritual Seeds
1. Plant God's Word in your children's hearts.
2. Teach your children that they can always seek the Lord, no matter where they are or what they have done. He is only a prayer away.
3. No one is ever too young or too old to invite the Holy Spirit to live in their heart.

Our Beautiful World Reflects the Glory of God

Lesson 11: Isaiah 45

The Lord spoke through Isaiah, "I made the earth and created man on it; it was my hands that stretched out the heavens, and I commanded all their host" (Isa. 45:12).

"For thus says the LORD, who created the heavens (he is God!), who formed the earth and made it (he established it; he did not create it empty, he formed it to be inhabited!): 'I am the LORD, and there is no other'" (Isa. 45:18).

Our world is beautiful in every way, and we should instill in our children an appreciation for God's incredible world and help them realize how every facet of our world interacts for the welfare of all. For example, clouds form when water evaporates, and then that water returns to earth as rain, snow, or hail, enabling plants and animals to live. Nature truly reflects the glory of God.

Our Heavenly Father also gives us spiritual water, His Holy Spirit, when we invite Him into our hearts. As rain cleanses nature on the outside, the Holy Spirit cleanses us on the inside. May each family member seek a spiritual cleansing.

Plant Spiritual Seeds

1. Teach your children the song "God's Beautiful World" (you can search for it on the Internet), and help them develop an awe for their Creator.
2. Sense God's love for you as you gaze upon His beautiful world.
3. Care for God's creation, and please the *Master Gardener*.

He Is the Potter; We Are the Clay

Lesson 12: Isaiah 64

"But now, O Lord, you are our Father; we are the clay, and you are our potter; we are *all* the work of your hand" (emphasis added) (Isa. 64:8).

Everyone needs to stay moldable, like fresh clay, allowing their Heavenly Father to continually remold and use them daily. A favorite song of many is "Have Thine Own Way, Lord" written by Adelaide A. Pollard in 1907. There is a sweet story behind its lyrics.

Adelaide, disappointed she did not have the funds to go to Africa as a missionary, attended a prayer service where she overheard an elderly woman pray, "It's all right, Lord. It doesn't matter what You bring into our lives, just have Your own way with us." The prayer of that elderly woman and the verses below from Jeremiah inspired Adelaide to compose the hymn "Have Thine Own Way, Lord."

> *The word that came to Jeremiah from the* Lord*: "Arise, and go down to the potter's house, and there I will let you hear my words." So I went down to the potter's house, and there he was working at his wheel. And the vessel he was making of clay was spoiled in the potter's hand, and he reworked it into another vessel, as it seemed good to the potter to do.*
>
> *Then the word of the* Lord *came to me: "O house of Israel, can I not do with you as this potter has done? declares the* Lord*. Behold, like the clay in the potter's hand, so are you in my hand, O house of Israel."*
>
> —Jer. 18:1–6

Adelaide wrote all four stanzas of "Have Thine Own Way, Lord" that very night following the prayer meeting. Below are the lyrics for stanzas one and four:

> Have Thine own way, Lord! Have Thine own way!
> Thou art the Potter, I am the clay.
> Mold me and make me, wash me just now;
> As in Thy presence, humbly I bow.
>
> Have Thine own way, Lord! Have Thine own way!
> Hold o'er my being absolute sway!
> Fill with Thy Spirit 'till all shall see
> Christ only, always, living in me.[8]

Plant Spiritual Seeds

1. Allow the Lord to remold you daily as you seek to do His will.
2. Sing with your children "Have Thine Own Way, Lord" (search for the video on the Internet).

Jeremiah

When God called Jeremiah, a teenager, to preach repentance to the Judeans, Israel had already fallen to the Assyrians, and the Judeans were facing deportation to Babylonia if they didn't repent. What a challenge for such a young man! For 40 years, Jeremiah attempted to change the hearts of God's people, but they completely ignored him, and their deportation was fast approaching. When that dreadful day arrived, Jeremiah wept as he watched the Babylonians gather their first group of deportees. Two more groups would be deported to Babylonia, leaving only Jeremiah and a handful of Judeans in Judah. Then such extreme anguish came upon Jeremiah as he watched the total destruction of Jerusalem, including Solomon's Temple, that he became known as the Weeping Prophet.

Those exiled in Babylonia would return in 70 years, and the remnant that was left behind would stay spiritually strong through Jeremiah's leadership.

God Had a Plan for Jeremiah's Life, and He Has a Plan for Us

Lesson 1: Jeremiah 1

> Now the word of the LORD came to me [Jeremiah], saying,
> "Before I formed you in the womb I **knew you**,
> **and before you were born I consecrated you;**
> I appointed you a prophet to the nations" (emphasis added).
> —Jer. 1:4–5

Jeremiah spoke:
 "Ah, Lord GOD! Behold, I do not know how to speak, for I am only a youth." But the LORD said to me,

> "Do not say, 'I am only a youth';
> for to all to whom I send you, you shall go,
> and whatever I command you, you shall speak.
> Do not be afraid of them,
> for **I am with you** to deliver you,
> declares the LORD" (emphasis added).
> —Jer. 1:6–8

Jeremiah balked when God called him to become a prophet because he lacked confidence and questioned his ability to fulfill God's plan for his life. But he would soon learn that God compensates for one's weaknesses. Jeremiah, with God's help, made a concerted effort to draw the Judeans back to their Heavenly Father. Oh, how he wanted them to embrace God Almighty.

Even though the Judeans refused to repent and return to their Heavenly Father, Jeremiah fulfilled God's plan for his life. I believe that on the Day of Judgment, he will hear God say, "Well done, good and faithful servant" (Matt. 25:21).

Often when we seek to serve our Heavenly Father, we, like Jeremiah, also run into difficulties. But keep your head up because Satan always undermines anyone's attempt to serve the Lord. When God calls you, step forward and serve Him. My choosing to write a parenting guide has not been easy, but I was motivated to keep moving forward because I did not want to give Satan the victory. The turning point in my endeavor occurred one Sunday while attending Watermark Church in Dallas, Texas. The preacher, Todd Wagner, concluded his sermon, offered the closing prayer, and then, for no apparent reason, looked out at the congregation and proclaimed, "Every year your writing is getting better." As tears welled up in my eyes, I asked my husband, "Did you hear that?" He said, "Yes!" The music began, and the people began to leave. I left blessed and encouraged.

Be willing to sacrifice your own pleasures to meet the needs in God's kingdom. Your labor of love has eternal value.

Plant Spiritual Seeds

1. Walk only through the doors the Lord opens.
2. Pray this prayer with your family: "Lord, you know us. You know everything about each one of us. Here we are; use us for Your glory."
3. Remember, God enjoys taking those who are weak and giving them the ability to succeed.
4. Parenting a child to walk with the Lord is a powerful mission from God.

America, Don't Ignore God
Lesson 2: Jeremiah 5

When the Judeans refused to listen to Jeremiah, they were, in reality, refusing to listen to God who had given them many opportunities to repent and return to Him. Each time, they had refused. Now, their opportunity to repent was over, and they were on the verge of *divine destruction*.

God spoke strong words through Jeremiah: "As you have forsaken me and served foreign gods in your land, so you shall serve foreigners in a land that is not yours. . . . Your sins have kept good from you" (Jer. 5:19, 25). Jeremiah's attempt to turn Judah back to God was not in vain, however, because America can learn from Judah's mistake and choose to heed God's Ten Commandments and walk in His ways. As mentioned earlier in this book, every country that leaves God out of the equation will eventually be disciplined. America's spiritual foundation has weakened, but it is not too late for us to repent and reestablish our Christian heritage.

Years ago, First Lady Nancy Reagan initiated a campaign called the War on Drugs. Schools began to teach children to say no to drugs, and the program thrived in giving many children a predetermined mindset to say no when offered drugs.

Children need that same mindset to say no to lying, stealing, cursing, coveting, murdering, living immorally, and worshiping idols. In similar fashion, children need to say yes to obeying their parents, loving God with all their hearts, and loving their neighbors as themselves. In the early days of America, children read the Bible in their classrooms, and teachers embedded godly behavior and integrity in their hearts. Do you remember when a handshake was all it took to seal a deal? What happened?

We and our children need to stay on the straight and narrow path that leads to Heaven. To keep America a nation of strong, upstanding citizens with integrity, take time to train your children to walk in the ways of the Lord.

Americans, wake up, or we, too, will reap what we have sown.

Plant Spiritual Seeds

1. Pray that our country returns to God. Remember, God will bless any country if its people walk with Him.
2. Encourage your schools to join with parents and teach the Ten Commandments.
3. May all children seek their Heavenly Father, live morally, exhibit integrity, be truthful, extend kindness toward others, and, most importantly, forgive others as God has forgiven them.
4. Encourage your school's librarian to read stories that teach integrity to students. Marty Hinson, a retired librarian, did just that. What a blessing she provided her children and her country.

Your Heart Determines Your Rewards

Lesson 3: Jeremiah 17

"I the LORD *search the heart* and test the mind, to give every man according to his ways, according to the fruit of his deeds" (emphasis added) (Jer. 17:10).

Your Heavenly Father knows you very well. He knows where you are and what you are thinking. He searches your heart and knows the *motives behind* your actions. If you do something very kind and thoughtful but have alternative motives, He will *only see* your true motive. God cares more about a pure heart than actions.

Give your heart a good examination. Are you seeking to please the Lord or people?

> *Do not store up for yourselves treasurers on earth, where moths and vermin destroy, and where thieves break in and steal. But store up for yourselves treasurers in heaven, where moths and vermin do not destroy, and where thieves do not break in and steal. For where your treasure is, there your heart will be also.*
>
> —Matt. 6:19–21 NIV

Plant Spiritual Seeds

1. Remember, your motives are more important to God than what you say or do.
2. He can read our hearts and minds.

3. May our Heavenly Father ignite labors of love toward others through us. Ann, one of my Sunday school girls, sought God's help as she shopped for a nursing home patient's Christmas gift. God put it on her heart to buy bath powder. She did, and her lady was *thrilled*. Seek God's help whenever you shop for others.

May Each Generation Be Spiritually Strong

Lesson 4: Jeremiah 29

Jeremiah was not the only prophet who beseeched the Judeans to repent—there were numerous prophets. But after 100 years, sin was still so rampant in Judah that God had the Babylonians discipline the nation He loved. It began with the Babylonians taking captive the most promising Judeans.

God spoke through King Zedekiah, "Bow your neck under the yoke of the king of Babylon; serve him and his people, and you will live" (Jer. 27:12 NIV). Three groups were taken to Babylonia. Next, the Babylonians attacked those remaining in Judah. Many of them were slaughtered during the attacks or died from famine or disease. A small remnant, including *Jeremiah*, remained in Judah. This situation was ordained by God because the Judeans were sinful rebels.

Then God, through Jeremiah, sent a letter to those exiled in Babylonia, telling them to thrive while in Babylonia—have children, plant gardens, build homes for your families, marry, and have sons and daughters who will also marry and have sons and daughters. This reminded me of Israel's time-out in Egypt where it grew into a great nation. Now, God is orchestrating the rebuilding of Judah through a time-out in Babylonia.

God penned another letter to them through Jeremiah.

> *For thus says the* L%ORD*: When seventy years are completed for Babylon, I will visit you, and I will fulfill to you my promise and bring you back to this place.* **For I know the plans I**

> *have for you, declares the* LORD, *plans for welfare and not for evil, to give you a future and a hope.* Then you will call upon me and come and pray to me, and I will hear you. You will seek me and find me, when you seek me with all your heart. I will be found by you, declares the LORD, and I will restore your fortunes and gather you from all the nations and all the places where I have driven you, declares the LORD, and I will bring you back to the place from which I sent you into exile (emphasis added).
>
> —Jer. 29:10–14

From the second group of deportees, God called Ezekiel as a prophet (preacher) to encourage the Judeans to return to God and forgo their rebellious ways (Ezek. 2:3–5). After years of preaching and pleading with the Judeans to repent, Ezekiel succeeded; the Judeans reconnected with their Heavenly Father and were no longer sinful rebels worshiping idols.

The Babylonian exile was, in reality, a 70-year *spiritual time-out* for the nation of Judah. It took an *abundance* of spiritual food (70 years' worth) for the nation to develop hearts for God with a desire to walk in His ways.

This story provides a great parenting lesson for us today. Learn from Judah's mistake, and as you raise your children, provide an abundance of spiritual food, enabling them to stand strong, obey God's commandments, and seek to live godly lives. We do not want our children labeled sinful rebels, nor do we want them to suffer serious consequences.

When your children exhibit even a hint of disobedience, step forward and offer spiritual food. If they do not change their ways, discipline. They also need to stand strong when facing temptations. Parents and children alike need to pray and read His Word or a devotional book daily to maintain their spiritual strength and to bond with Him.

I have a special place in our house—called my chair—where I have my quiet times with Him. Let your children select a special place to seek and receive their spiritual food. In their special place, provide younger children with a children's Bible, a Bible storybook, and a biblical coloring book. Have preschoolers look through their storybook with their stuffed animal and choose a story to read at bedtime when you can nurture them spiritually. Older children can prepare their own special places. In their special place, they need a Bible, a devotional book, and a sack of Scripture memorization cards. Together, seek verses to memorize from the Sermon on the Mount (Matt. 5, 6, 7) the Psalms, Proverbs, and the Gospels (Matthew, Mark, Luke, and John).

Every time children or teenagers spend time with their Heavenly Father, their spiritual foundations are strengthened.

Take your children and teenagers to church. There, they will receive additional spiritual food that will enrich their lives and strengthen their integrity.

When children grow up knowing right from wrong, *they will bring honor to their Heavenly Father and give peace and joy to their parents.* They are truly on the pathway to Heaven. During their spiritual development, the day will come when they will want to invite Jesus to live in their hearts. Pray for that special day.

If a generation doesn't have a strong spiritual foundation, they probably will not bond with their Heavenly Father, and their country is more likely to drift away from the Lord and become spiritual rebels like the Judeans who needed discipline and spiritual nourishment. Never forget the fate of the Judeans—70 years in captivity—because the country ignored God.

May your country not repeat Judah's fate.

Plant Spiritual Seeds

1. Meet the needs of the next generation by nurturing the present generation to walk and bond with God Almighty. May your family invite the Holy Spirit to live in their hearts.
2. As it is important to obey God, it is equally important to obey parents.
3. Spiritual nourishment on the inside begets godly behavior on the outside.
4. May our children's special places draw them closer to their Heavenly Father.
5. Set an example for your children, and seek the Lord daily.
6. May your walk mirror the dreams you have for your children.

Lamentations

The word *lament* means to cry out in grief or to mourn. Lamentations is a lament, written by Jeremiah, describing the heavy-heartedness that the remnant in Judah experienced as they watched the demolition of Jerusalem. It began after the third group, made up of 10,000 Judeans, was deported to Babylonia. The destruction of Jerusalem, especially Solomon's Temple, made it very clear to the remnant that sin has consequences.

Our Heavenly Father would never choose to destroy Jerusalem or Solomon's Temple. But God had *no other option* but to *discipline* the nation He loved because they refused to repent.

Parents also suffer when their children go astray. Administering discipline is indicative of parental love. Like the Judeans, children often fail to change their behaviors, even after discipline. What grief parents experience over a rebellious, sinful child!

May we and our children faithfully *obey God's Word* throughout our lives and not fail to pass His Word down to the next generation.

During Difficult Times, Seek Your Heavenly Father

Lesson: Lamentations 5

The Judeans' waywardness made discipline inevitable. Their leaving Judah was emotional, sad, and painful because they had to vacate their homes and travel to an unknown country.

> *Remember, O Lord, what has befallen us;*
> * look, and see our disgrace!*
> *Our inheritance has been turned over to strangers,*
> * our homes to foreigners.*
> *We have become orphans, fatherless;*
> * our mothers are like widows.*
> *We must pay for the water we drink;*
> * the wood we get must be bought.*
> *Our pursuers are at our necks;*
> * we are weary; we are given no rest.*
>
> —Lam. 5:1–5

Dr. Gene A. Getz, a Bible scholar, gives us directives: "When we are enduring discipline, we should not turn away from the Lord, but turn toward Him for healing and intimate fellowship with Him."[9]

It often takes harsh discipline to get a nation like Judah or an individual back on the straight and narrow path. However, harsh punishment can change a nation or a person's life, as was the case with Erik Leslie.

DURING DIFFICULT TIMES, SEEK YOUR HEAVENLY FATHER

Erik, a Young Life leader, and his girlfriend were talking to her parents while he was driving. He became distracted and had an unintentional one-car accident that took his girlfriend's life and forced the state to charge him with involuntary manslaughter. After the accident, authorities tested him for alcohol and drugs and found a trace amount of marijuana in his system. He was sentenced to 500 hours of community service. After reflecting on this sentence, he went before the judge and asked permission to speak and encourage youths to refrain from driving while under the influence of alcohol or drugs or while using their cell phones. The judge accepted his request, and Erik diligently completed his community service. That wise judge allowed him to change lives instead of pick up trash. After completing his 500 hours, he continued speaking for an additional 300 hours and became an excellent spokesperson.

The effect of Erik's community service cannot be determined, and we can only imagine how many lives have been saved and how many wrecks have been avoided because of his passion to share his horrendous experience with others. Erik's harsh punishment had positive results.

Judges, be creative, and choose community services that will correct the misbehavior and benefit humankind. Erik's heart was changed, and countless youths became responsible drivers.

Although Erik leaned on the Lord while performing his community service, a year later, he became depressed and most likely had a form of PTSD (post-traumatic stress disorder). He worked through his depression and finished college with a degree in sports and performance psychology. He has had a successful career on a military base, counseling those who suffer from PTSD and other emotional problems. His community service changed the course of his life.

Scripture helped Erik through his troubled times and still guides his life today. One of the most meaningful verses during those dark days was "I [God] will turn the darkness before them into light, the rough places into level ground" (Isa. 42:16). This verse still hangs as a plaque in Erik's home.

Ultimately, Erik's harsh discipline through the judicial system had a positive outcome: *he grew spiritually* and chose his vocation through his countless speaking engagements. Most likely, many accidents and deaths were prevented.

The Judeans also benefitted from their punishment. After 70 years in exile, they developed hearts for God and were prepared to rebuild Jerusalem, including Solomon's Temple.

Faithfully serving our Heavenly Father is a day-by-day decision. We need to seek His will for our lives and remember that Satan is always there to distract our efforts.

Plant Spiritual Seeds

1. When life hands you a lemon, make lemonade.
2. Wise discipline should *change behavior*, not just *punish misbehavior*. Erik's judge is to be commended.
3. May our families faithfully live God-pleasing lives.

Ezekiel

Ezekiel was in the second group of deportees. After living in Babylonia for five years, God called him as a prophet (preacher) to those living near the Chebar Canal. Later, a third group of deportees numbering 10,000 joined Ezekiel, creating a nice-sized Jewish community in Babylonia. There, Ezekiel nourished them spiritually.

The exile strengthened Judah instead of disabling her. What Satan meant for evil, God meant for good. Ezekiel totally understood God's desire for the Judeans to return to Him.

> *I will remove the heart of stone [idolatry] from their flesh and give them a heart of flesh [hearts that love God], that they may walk in my statutes and keep my rules and obey them. And they shall be my people, and I will be their God.*
> —Ezek. 11:19–20

Ezekiel made it clear to the Judeans that their deportation constituted needed discipline; God had done no wrong.

God gave Ezekiel many interesting visions to redirect the Judeans from worshiping idols to trusting and worshiping Him. The Judeans responded to his teaching and embraced their Heavenly Father. When the 70-year captivity was over, idolatry was no longer an issue—the Judeans were seeking to please their Heavenly Father. Their hearts were indeed changed. Harsh punishment had brought great results.

Do not let your children's behavior get out of hand. If they do not obey you, they probably will not obey their Heavenly Father or any other authoritative figure. God allowed the Babylonian exile to bring His people back to living a God-pleasing life.

Plant God's Word in the Next Generation

Lesson 1: Ezekiel 12

Years before the Babylonian exile, King Josiah encouraged the Judeans to draw close to the Lord by hearing and adhering to Scripture (page 138). Throughout the Babylonian exile, God had Ezekiel impress upon the Jewish nation, just as Josiah had in a previous generation, the importance of knowing and obeying God's Word. God spoke these words through Ezekiel: "Son of man, you dwell in the midst of a rebellious house, who have eyes to see, but see not, who have ears to hear, but hear not, for they are a rebellious house" (Ezek. 12:2).

The Judeans learned and parents today need to learn how vital it is that the next generation is grounded in the Word of God. Parents, take this responsibility seriously, never stop planting spiritual seeds in the hearts of all children, and choose to give spiritual gifts to one and all.

May each family member be able to proclaim, "I have hidden your word in my heart that I might not sin against you" (Ps. 119:11 NIV). Initiate a Scripture memorization program in your home or church. Those who memorize a verse each week will have 52 verses planted in their hearts by year's end. After the second year, they will have more than a hundred Scriptures tucked away to lead them on the pathway of righteousness.

Spiritual growth is invaluable—children need to know God's Word before they can keep His Word. Parents will enjoy a sense of security knowing their children are grounded in the Word.

Plant Spiritual Seeds

1. Encourage Scripture memorization in your home. There are many life-changing verses to memorize from the Sermon on the Mount as well as in the Psalms and Proverbs. Do not fail to memorize the Ten Commandments and the Lord's Prayer (Matt. 6:9–13). One week, you might even memorize a Scripture song such as the one from Ephesians 4:32. Let family members take turns selecting memory verses. Remember, offering rewards encourages memorization.

2. An easy way to memorize is to act out Scripture. For example, the motions for "The LORD is my strength and my song" (Exod. 15:2) might be "The LORD" (point up toward Heaven) "is my strength" (flex your muscles) "and my song" (place your fingers on your lips and then pull them away). Acting out a verse is fun and brings success. Learn Scripture references as well.

3. Play charades to review previously memorized Scripture.

Who Is Responsible for Your Sins?
Lesson 2: Ezekiel 18

The soul who sins shall die. The son shall not suffer for the iniquity of the father, nor the father suffer for the iniquity of the son. The righteousness of the righteous shall be upon himself, and the wickedness of the wicked shall be upon himself.
— Ezek. 18:20

We are all accountable for our sins. However, children will not be held accountable until God, who sees their hearts, deems them accountable.

Parents, choose to be a stepping stone instead of a stumbling block in your children's lives. Start by regularly taking them to church, remembering that merely taking them to church on Sunday is not enough. They need spiritual food from home as well.

Plant Spiritual Seeds

1. Diligently broadcast spiritual seeds into the *lives of everyone.*
2. Youth need to begin their teenage years spiritually strong in order to stand firm when Satan tempts them to sin.
3. Invite unchurched families to visit your church, and encourage your children to invite their friends not only to church on Sundays but also to Bible school and summer church camps. When friends walk with the Lord, everyone benefits.
4. Remember, children will reap what you sow into their hearts, be it good or bad.
5. When Ezekiel planted a multiplicity of spiritual seeds in the hearts of the Judeans, they became spiritually strong.

Daniel

The first group of Judeans deported to Babylonia included Daniel, his friends, and the most promising Judeans.

The first six chapters of Daniel focus on Daniel and his friends who lived exemplary lives while captive in Babylonia.

Through these men's lives, we have three parenting lessons:

1. Take care of your body.
1. Keep God's commandments.
2. Trust God even in a lion's den.

The last six chapters of Daniel are devoted to end-time prophecies that will usher in Jesus's return to earth.

Take Care of Your Body

Lesson 1: Daniel 1–2

In Babylon, "Daniel resolved that he would not defile himself with the king's food, or with the wine that he drank" (Dan. 1:8).

Daniel asked the chief official if Shadrach, Meshach, Abednego, and he could have only *vegetables and water* for 10 days. After that period, he wanted the chief official to compare their health with the other young men who ate the royal food of King Nebuchadnezzar. Ten days later, Daniel, Shadrach, Meshach, and Abednego did look healthier and better nourished, and the chief official put *every young man on Daniel's diet* instead of the royal food.

Because of their examples, God gave Daniel and his three friends knowledge and understanding of all kinds of literature and learning, and Daniel could also interpret visions and dreams.

Once night, King Nebuchadnezzar had a dream he did not understand, so he called for his wise men to interpret it. Unable to do so, the wise men suggested that Daniel, the exiled Judean, might be able to interpret it. Daniel stood before King Nebuchadnezzar and proceeded to describe his dream.

> *You saw, O king, and behold, a great image. This image, mighty and of exceeding brightness, stood before you, and its appearance was frightening. The head of this image was of fine gold, its chest and arms of silver, its middle and thighs of bronze, its legs of iron, its feet partly of iron and partly of clay.*
> —Dan. 2:31–33

Wow! That was exactly what the king had dreamed. Daniel then proceeded to interpret the dream. Through Daniel, God explained that each body part represented a world power. The golden head represented Babylonia, the current ruling nation, while the other metals represented future world powers. When Daniel correctly interpreted the dream, Nebuchadnezzar believed that Daniel's God truly was the Lord of lords.

> *Then the king gave Daniel high honors and many great gifts, and made him ruler over the whole province of Babylon and chief prefect [administrator] over all the wise men of Babylon.*
> —Dan. 2:48

Plant Spiritual Seeds

1. Like Daniel and his friends, seek to please God rather than people (Dan. 1–2).
2. Remember, your body is the temple of the Holy Spirit, so eat healthy food. Glorify God by what you eat as well as what you say and do.
3. Obedience to God brings God's blessings. God blessed Daniel with the ability to interpret dreams and gave him knowledge and understanding of all kinds of literature and learning.

Shadrach, Meshach, and Abednego Refused to Worship Idols

Lesson 2: Daniel 3

The Bible clearly states that we should not worship idols. However, King Nebuchadnezzar encouraged idol worship after making a golden image of himself that was 90 feet tall and 9 feet wide, resembling the image in his dream. After the statue was completed:

> And the herald proclaimed aloud, "You are commanded, O peoples, nations, and languages, that when you hear the sound of the horn, pipe, lyre, trigon, harp, bagpipe, and every kind of music, you are to fall down and worship the golden image that King Nebuchadnezzar has set up."
> —Dan. 3:4–5

Those who refused to bow down and worship Nebuchadnezzar's statue were thrown into the fiery furnace. Shadrach, Meshach, and Abednego refused to follow this decree, and their disobedience infuriated King Nebuchadnezzar. He summoned them and warned them that they had two choices: either worship his idol or face the blazing furnace.

The three men told the king that they still would not worship the golden image. Moreover, if the king threw them into the fire, they knew their God would be able to save them. But if He chose not to, they still would not worship the golden image.

Nebuchadnezzar ordered them thrown into the blaze, and God indeed performed a miracle in saving them. The fire did not harm their bodies, their hair was not singed, their robes remained pristine, and they did not even smell like smoke.

When God protected them, Nebuchadnezzar proclaimed:

> *Nebuchadnezzar answered and said, "Blessed be the God of Shadrach, Meshach, and Abednego, who has sent his angel and delivered his servants, who trusted in him, and set aside the king's command, and yielded up their bodies rather than serve and worship any god except their own God.*
>
> —Dan. 3:28

Nebuchadnezzar then gave a decree that anyone who said anything against the God of Shadrach, Meshach, and Abednego would be cut into pieces, for the king now knew that *no other god could save in this way*. What a testimony these three men displayed for God! Their faithfulness brought them blessings from God.

Plant Spiritual Seeds

1. Read the story of Shadrach, Meshach, and Abednego to your children (Dan. 3:8–30).
2. Stand up for God as Shadrach, Meshach, and Abednego did.
3. Never worship idols—worship only God Almighty.
4. Remind your children to set a godly example at school.

Daniel Trusted God Even in a Lion's Den

Lesson 3: Daniel 6

After the deaths of King Nebuchadnezzar and his son Belshazzar, Babylonia was under the control of the Medes. The new king, Darius, appointed Daniel and two other men as administrators. When Daniel had distinguished himself above the other two, the king asked Daniel to rule over the entire kingdom. Naturally, this immensely upset the other administrators, so they devised a plan to get Daniel arrested. They knew no one would believe any charges brought against Daniel unless they could devise a plan that forced Daniel to choose between the laws of the land and God's law.

The men went to the king and asked him to issue an edict stating that anyone who prayed to a god or man besides the king would be thrown into the lions' den. King Darius put this decree into writing. The administrators knew Daniel would never obey this decree and closely watched Daniel until they saw him praying to his God. They ran to King Darius and reported, "He [Daniel] got down on his knees three times a day and prayed and gave thanks before his God, as he had done previously" (Dan. 6:10).

When the king heard this, he was greatly distressed because he actually liked Daniel. But unable to find a way to save him, King Darius proceeded with the edict, and the men came and cast Daniel into the lions' den. King Darius sadly spoke to Daniel: "May your God, whom you serve continually, deliver you!" (Dan. 6:16).

Unable to sleep the entire night, King Darius got up at dawn and ran to the lions' den. He called out to Daniel, fearing that he might not answer because the lions had ravaged him. However, Daniel did answer. "O king,

DANIEL TRUSTED GOD EVEN IN A LION'S DEN

live forever! My God sent his angel and shut the lions' mouths, and they have not harmed me, because I was found blameless before him; and also before you, O king, I have done no harm" (Dan. 6:21–22).

The jubilant king ordered that Daniel be lifted out of the den. The lions had not even scratched Daniel—God had kept him safe. Why did the lions not touch Daniel? Because God heard and answered Daniel's prayer for protection. Why did God answer his prayer? Daniel *always* chose to do *what was right*, which made him righteous. Therefore, God answered Daniel's prayer and shut the lions' mouths.

Always remember, "The prayer of a *righteous person* is powerful and effective" (emphasis added) (James 5:16 NIV).

> *Then King Darius wrote to all the peoples, nations, and languages that dwelt in all the earth: "Peace be multiplied to you. I make a decree, that in all my royal dominion people are to tremble and fear before the God of Daniel,*
>
>> *for he is the living God,*
>>   *enduring forever;*
>> *his kingdom shall **never be destroyed**,*
>>   *and his dominion shall be to the end.*
>> *He delivers and rescues;*
>>   *he works signs and wonders*
>>   *in heaven and on earth,*
>> *he who has saved Daniel*
>>   *from the power of the lions"* (emphasis added).
>
> —Dan. 6:25–27

After that, Daniel continued to prosper during the remainder of King Darius's reign and the reign of the next king, Cyrus, the Persian.

Plant Spiritual Seeds

1. Read the story of Daniel in the lions' den to your children (Dan. 6). Encourage them to always choose to do what is right, like Daniel. It will make them righteous, and God will hear their prayers.
2. Remember, righteousness precedes answered prayers.

3. Ask your children what lions they are facing. Together, draw into His presence, and seek His help and protection.
4. As a family, determine ways to let your light shine for the Lord in your community and at school. Be an ambassador for your Heavenly Father. May your walk and talk bring glory to Him.

End Times: Separation of the Sheep and the Goats

Lesson 4: Daniel 12

The last six chapters of Daniel are devoted to end-time prophecies concerning events that will usher in the return of Christ to earth. When that time comes, Jesus will separate the sheep from the goats.

> *At that time shall arise Michael, the great prince [angel] who has charge of your people. And there shall be a time of trouble, such as never has been since there was a nation till that time. But at that time your people shall be delivered, everyone whose* name *shall be found* **written in the book**. *And many of those who sleep in the dust of the earth shall awake, some to everlasting life, and some to shame and everlasting contempt. And those who are wise shall shine like the brightness of the sky above; and those who turn many to righteousness, like the stars forever and ever. But you, Daniel, shut up the words and seal the book, until the time of the end. Many shall run to and fro, and knowledge shall increase* (emphasis added).
>
> —Dan. 12:1–4

In Matthew 25, Jesus further expounded on this prophecy:

> *When the Son of Man [Jesus] comes in his glory, and all the angels with him, then he will sit on his glorious throne. Before him will be gathered all the nations, and he will separate people one from another as a shepherd separates the sheep from the goats. And he will place the sheep on his right, but the goats on the left. Then the King will say to those on his right, "Come, you who are blessed by my Father, inherit the kingdom prepared for you from the foundation of the world. . . ." Then he will say to those on his left, "Depart from me, you cursed, into the eternal fire prepared for the devil and his angels."*
>
> —Matt. 25:31–34, 41

Plant Spiritual Seeds

1. Prepare today for eternity by inviting the Holy Spirit into your heart.
2. After we receive the Holy Spirit within, our names are written in the Lamb's Book of Life.

Hosea

Hosea became a prophet in Israel 28 years before the Israelites fell to Assyria in 722 BC. The Israelites were deported indefinitely.

Prior to Israel's fall, times were prosperous, and people were self-centered. Hosea attempted to get the Israelites to repent and return to their Heavenly Father, but their self-centeredness caused them to drift further and further away from their Heavenly Father and into idol worship.

Avoid Idolatry and Adultery

Lesson 1: Hosea 1

God wanted Hosea to understand how painful it was to see His people, the Israelites, reaching out to idols instead of to Him. So He said to Hosea, "Go, take to yourself a wife of whoredom [unfaithfulness] and have children of whoredom, for the land commits great whoredom by forsaking the LORD" (Hosea 1:2). Hosea would come to understand that physical and spiritual adultery are similar.

Hosea listened to God and married an adulterous wife. He then understood God's hurt and pain when the Israelites left Him to worship idols. In a similar manner, Hosea's wife, Gomer, gave him much agony when she put her lovers before him.

Even though Israel was unfaithful to God, God still loved Israel. And even though Gomer was unfaithful to Hosea, Hosea still loved and cared for Gomer.

The book of Hosea stresses the need to keep these two commandments: "You shall have no other gods before me" (Exod. 20:3) and "You shall not commit adultery" (Exod. 20:14).

Plant Spiritual Seeds

1. Exemplify a godly marriage before your children.
2. Never worship idols.

Forgiveness Is Essential to Walk a Godly Path

Lesson 2: Hosea 3

The Lord spoke again to Hosea, "Go again, love a woman who is loved by another man and is an adulteress, even as the Lord loves the children of Israel, though they turn to other gods and love cakes of raisins" (Hosea 3:1).

God and Hosea both had a desire and willingness to forgive and return evil with kindness. Forgiveness is necessary in all relationships and is so essential that even the Lord's Prayer (Matt. 6:9–13) stresses the importance of forgiveness: "And forgive us our debts, as we also have forgiven our debtors" (Matt. 6:12). We should graciously forgive others as God has graciously forgiven us.

Teach your children to love and forgive others as they would want others to love and forgive them. If God and Hosea could forgive such serious breaches, we surely should be able to forgive one another.

Plant Spiritual Seeds

1. Love and forgive others as God loved and forgave the Israelites and as Hosea loved and forgave Gomer.
2. Forgiveness is essential to walking a godly path.
3. Encourage your children to forgive those who wrong them. "For if you forgive others their trespasses, your heavenly Father will also forgive you, but if you do not forgive others their trespasses, neither will your Father forgive your trespasses" (Matt. 6:14–15).
4. If your child has hurt a friend, have him or her verbally seek forgiveness or write a note seeking forgiveness.

Joel

Very little is known about Joel besides the fact that he was the son of Pethuel and he served Judah as a prophet preaching repentance, but to no avail. The Judeans brought the locust attack on themselves because of their sinful lifestyles. Immediately after the attack, the country lamented, put on their sackcloth, fasted, and prayed for forgiveness.

The locust invasion constituted discipline from God. It *completely* wiped out all the grasses, plants, trees, crops, and even seeds, leaving Judah totally void of vegetation and creating a national famine. Joel compared this locust invasion to a powerful army with an unbelievable number of men marching across the land, destroying everything in sight. The aftermath resembled a destructive fire. After the locust attack, Judah needed total restoration. Its people needed spiritual restoration, and the land needed vegetative restoration.

To get a visual of a locust attack, search the Internet for a video of a locust attack. Wow! Locusts are unbelievably destructive. God's discipline of Judah was to teach all people to remain in tune with their Heavenly Father during times *of prosperity* and in *times of need*.

The Locust Attack on Judah and Future Prophecy

Lesson 1: Joel 1–3

God tells us to share the story of the locust attack with our children: "Tell your children of it, and let your children tell their children, and their children to another generation" (Joel 1:3).

After the locust attack completely destroyed Judah, God through Joel told the priests to put on sackcloth, lament, and then "declare a holy fast; call a sacred assembly . . . and cry out to the Lord" (Joel 1:14 NIV). Joel had recognized a deeper meaning behind the locust attack. Since Judah's *spiritual weakness* was the culprit, Joel stepped forward and preached repentance. He called on the people to "rend your hearts and not your garments. Return to the Lord your God, for he is gracious and merciful, slow to anger, and abounding in steadfast love; and he relents over disaster" (Joel 2:13). Joel assured the people that if they repented, God would again bless their land. Wisely, the Judeans *chose* to repent.

The locusts might *not* have swarmed Judah if the Judeans had stood firm in their faith. Yet when they failed, God with His unconditional love for them, willingly forgave and forgot their wrongdoings.

God has unconditional love for us as well. Seek His forgiveness.

The story of the locust attack prepares future generations for the Day of the Lord when Jesus returns and raptures His family to Heaven. Those *left behind* will immediately become aware of their gross mistakes, ignoring God's invitation to follow Him. "Let all the inhabitants of the land tremble, for the day of the LORD is coming; it is near, a day of darkness and gloom, a day of clouds and thick darkness!" (Joel 2:1–2). Joel then describes the turmoil that would ensue on earth.

Those who are left behind need to realize that they were left behind because they did not embrace their Heavenly Father. God is waiting for the wayward to reach out, seek Him, repent, and return to Him like the Judeans did after the locust attack. God cares for each person as loving parents care for a repentant child.

Plant Spiritual Seeds

1. Share the story of the locust attack with your children, and explain why they need to be walking with the Lord *before* the Day of the Lord arrives in order to experience the rapture. Those left behind will face trials and tribulations. Yet they can choose to seek the Lord even during those dark days.
2. Our children need to learn that ungodly behavior does have consequences. If your children do wrong, encourage them to pray, repent, and seek God's forgiveness. Their sincerity will determine if they need discipline.
3. Countries as well as individuals are responsible for their actions. Both need to stay spiritually strong and obey their Heavenly Father in order to avoid discipline.
4. God is gracious, compassionate, slow to anger, and abounding in love, but there is a tipping point when discipline becomes inevitable.

Have a Heart for God's Family, Israel

Lesson 2: Joel 3

During the end times, God's people will return to Israel, and God will wage His final war against all His enemies.

> *Multitudes, multitudes,*
> *in the valley of decision!*
> *For the day of the LORD is near*
> *in the valley of decision.*
> *The sun and the moon are darkened,*
> *and the stars withdraw their shining.*
>
> *The LORD roars from Zion,*
> *and utters his voice from Jerusalem,*
> *and the heavens and the earth quake.*
> *But the LORD is a refuge to his people,*
> *a stronghold to the people of Israel.*
>
> —Joel 3:14–16

Have wisdom, and show kindness toward God's people, Israel. God spoke to Abraham, "I will bless those who bless you, and him who dishonors you I will curse, and in you all the families of the earth shall be blessed" (Gen. 12:3). Imagine God's agony during World War II when the Nazis set up concentration camps and orchestrated the annihilation of approximately six million Jews. The Holocaust truly was a travesty.

We honor God when we respect His people.

Plant Spiritual Seeds

1. Invite the Holy Spirit into your heart, and become grafted into the family of God.
2. Satan is the one responsible for evil in this world. Choose to please your Heavenly Father, not Satan.
3. Have a heart for God's people. Put Israel on your prayer list.
4. There are many occasions when a natural catastrophe follows sinful actions. Pick up the book *As America Has Done to Israel* by John P. McTernan. It is the history of how people's negative actions toward God and His people have coincidentally resulted in natural catastrophes in America. Knowing that natural catastrophes can cause many deaths is another reason why we should all be ready to meet our Creator on any given day.

Amos

Amos was a shepherd from Judah when God called him away from his flock to travel to Israel and deliver a message of repentance. En route, he preached repentance to every nation and city because they were all living in sin and needed to repent. Those nations and cities included Damascus, Gaza, Tyre, Edom, Amon, Moab, Judah, and, of course, eventually Israel.

Each nation and city heard these same two pleas from God through Amos:

1. You did not return to me (Amos 4:9).
2. I will punish you for your transgressions (Amos 3:14).

Can repentance protect a country from devastation? Yes. Do repentant children need discipline? No. God and parents are kind and compassionate when it comes to offenses. When children change their behavior, parents breathe a sigh of relief.

Repentance not only strengthens your country, it also keeps divine discipline at bay.

Cities and Countries Reap What They Sow

Lesson: Amos 1, 3, 7, 9

God is our Heavenly Father. He is loving, kind, and patient, and desires that we live *godly* lives. In Amos, we read that God overlooked serious blunders made by eight nations/cities before He deemed it necessary to punish them. "For three transgressions of Damascus, and for four, I [God] will not revoke the punishment" (Amos 1:3). Since none of the eight nations/cities chose to repent, they all suffered severe consequences. "Israel shall surely go into exile [Assyria] away from its land" (Amos 7:17).

Every generation needs to diligently sow into the next generation the commandments and the ways of God. If they do, all is well. Conversely, if a generation ignores God, overlooking His commandments and rules for living, the next generation is in *great trouble*. Families, individuals, cities, and countries will always reap what they sow. Therefore, godly leadership within a family as well as in all levels of government is essential. Remember, when the Hebrew nation did not trust God to lead them safely into the Promised Land, God disciplined them. Those who were 20 years old or more would never be allowed to enter the Promised Land (Joshua and Caleb were exceptions), and those younger than 20 would enter after the older generation had died off in the wilderness. Review their story on page 50 ("Trust and Obedience Bring Success").

Nurture the next generation spiritually, and live exemplary lives before them. Sow an abundance of spiritual seeds in the hearts of *all* children, praying for a bountiful harvest that translates into a generational blessing—a nation of strong, godly citizens.

Do you believe that a town with a large number of active churches has fewer crimes than a city with only a few churches? If a country or city sows an abundance of spiritual seeds year after year, peace and tranquility will prevail to the extent that seeds have been sown.

God assured Amos that He would eventually restore Israel during the end times. "I will plant them on their land, and they shall never again be uprooted out of the land that I have given them, says the LORD your God" (Amos 9:15).

Plant Spiritual Seeds

1. Pray that your country and its leaders will follow the ways of the Lord.
2. Listen for God's voice, and when you hear it, obey.
3. Keep your country spiritually strong.
4. Obedience to God precedes blessings from God.
5. Here are some profound quotes from God:
   - "Be good, flee evil—and live!" (Amos 5:14 TLB).
   - "Hate evil and love the good" (Amos 5:15 TLB).
   - "I want to see a mighty flood of justice—a torrent of doing good" (Amos 5:24 TLB).
   - "Seek me—and live" (Amos 5:4 TLB).

Obadiah

The book of Obadiah is only 21 verses long, yet it contains a valuable lesson. It describes an unhealthy relationship between twin brothers: Esau and Jacob.

These two boys were the sons of Isaac and Rebekah and the grandsons of Abraham and Sarah. Esau's homeland was Edom, and Jacob's was Israel/Judah. The prophet Obadiah received a vision that foretold the total destruction of Edom because Esau's descendants cheered instead of helping Jacob's descendants fight off the Babylonians.

Refresh your memory by rereading their story (page 13).

Esau's and Jacob's families should have stayed connected through adversities. Without Edom's help, Judah was vulnerable and easily fell to the Babylonians.

Families today need to learn from the Edomites' mistake. Overlook wrongdoings, and choose to bond, support, and care for your family and your extended family.

Never Rejoice over Others' Misfortunes

Lesson: Obadiah 1

God spoke to the descendants of Esau about their homeland, Edom:

> Because of the violence done to your brother Jacob,
>   shame shall cover you,
>   and you shall be cut off **forever**.
> On the day that you stood aloof,
>   on the day that strangers carried off his wealth
> and foreigners entered his gates
>   and cast lots for Jerusalem,
>   you were like one of them.
> But do not gloat over the day of your brother
>   in the day of his misfortune;
> do not rejoice over the people of Judah
>   in the day of their ruin;
> do not boast
>   in the day of distress (emphasis added).
>
> —Obad. 1:10–12

The struggles between Esau's and Jacob's families ignited after Jacob, the younger son, received not only the family's birthright but also his father's blessing. To become the patriarch, Jacob would also need to obtain his father's blessings before he died. Rebekah helped Jacob disguise himself and deceive his father into thinking that he was Esau, thereby receiving the blessing. It was foreordained that Jacob would become the patriarch, but it should have been done God's way, not Rebekah's way. This deception separated the boys and their families. Later in life, the two reunited, but their families did not. The generational curse of *deception (lying)* had been established in Jacob's family. A different generational curse fell on Esau's family—*negative vibes against Jacob's family*. Because of these negative vibes, Esau's descendants refused to help Jacob's descendants fight off the Babylonians, causing God to cut off Esau's family forever.

Never rejoice when a brother, sister, or friend goes through unbearable circumstances. If anyone has been unkind to you, cheated you, or harmed you in any manner, realize that they are accountable to God. Overlooking an offense is the proper response.

Do not return evil with evil. Instead, return evil with kindness. Esau's heirs learned the hard way that "as you have done, it shall be done to you; your deeds shall return on your own head" (Obad. 1:15). Because Esau's family refused to overlook the deceptive ways of Jacob's family, Esau's family would eventually *lose their country permanently*.

Plant Spiritual Seeds

1. Generational curses are serious. Seek to lift generational curses off your family.
2. Make a concerted effort to maintain peace and harmony within your family.
3. Never return evil with evil. *Instead,* return evil with *kindness*. Be compassionate toward others, especially your siblings.
4. "Above all, love each other deeply, because love covers over a multitude of sins" (1 Pet. 4:8 NIV).

Jonah

It might be fun for your children and grandchildren to use their Bibles. There are 10 valuable lessons in the book of Jonah. Teach them to your children. Your amount of participation will be determined by the age of your children.

- Read the story of Jonah to your younger children, and together identify the 10 lessons found in the book of Jonah.
- Have your older children read and highlight Scriptures for each lesson, putting the Scripture reference below each lesson title.

Ten Lessons from the Book of Jonah

Read the book of Jonah, and highlight or mark Scriptures for each lesson. Write the Scripture references below the lesson's title.

Lesson 1: Obey Your Heavenly Father and Earthly Parents

    Scripture Reference: _____

- Obedience to your Heavenly Father and your parents is a commandment.

Jonah should have obeyed his Heavenly Father and gone to Nineveh instead of disobeying Him and taking the ship to Tarshish.

Lesson 2: Disobedience Brings Discipline

    Scripture Reference: _____

Jonah's disobedience to God resulted in a violent storm that could have destroyed the ship and its crew. Knowing that the storm was the result of his disobedience, Jonah told the crew to throw him overboard. After much hesitation, they did, and immediately the *storm subsided*. When those onboard saw the storm immediately subside, *they worshiped and received the God of Jonah*.

A large fish then swallowed Jonah, and three days later, it spewed him out to complete God's mission.

- If you disobey your earthly parents, repent or expect discipline.
- If you disobey your Heavenly Father, repent or expect discipline.
- Discipline can bring great results.

Lesson 3: The Miraculous Power of God

Scripture Reference: _____

- God controls all situations, from speaking a storm into existence to stilling a storm. He even protected Jonah in the belly of a fish for three days and three nights.

Lesson 4: The Power of Prayer

Scripture Reference: _____

- In the belly of the fish, Jonah prayed for help. His Heavenly Father responded and spewed him out onto dry ground. Jonah then made his way to Nineveh.

Lesson 5: The Importance of a Second Chance

Scripture Reference: _____

- God gave Jonah a second chance to preach repentance to the Ninevites. This time, Jonah obeyed. He needed a second chance, and frequently our children do as well.

Lesson 6: God Can Use One Person to Make a Big Difference

Scripture Reference: _____

- Jonah led the people of Nineveh to repent. Impress upon your children that God can use them to make a big difference. Encourage your children to be available.

Lesson 7: God Is Gracious, Merciful, Slow to Anger, and Abounding in Steadfast Love

Scripture Reference: _____

- God accepted the Ninevites' genuine repentance and had compassion on them. He did not destroy their city. We all need to extend mercy, compassion, and love toward others when they repent.

Lesson 8: Do Not Have a Pity Party

Scripture Reference: _____

- After the people repented, God did not destroy Nineveh. However, Jonah responded with a pity party. Why? He had been successful. He should have rejoiced.
- Parents, rejoice when your children repent, making discipline unnecessary. It is truly a milestone when children self-correct. Praise them.

Lesson 9: Rejoice When the Lord Saves Sinners

Scripture Reference: _____

- If any man is in Christ, he is a new creation. Rejoice!

Lesson 10: God Has a Plan for Your Life

Scripture Reference: _____

- Ask God to reveal His plan for your life. Is there someone who needs your help? Is there something He wants you to do? Daily, seek His plans for you.

Plant Spiritual Seeds

1. Does your child need a second chance?
2. Remind your children that God hears their prayers.
3. God is a God of miracles.
4. Prayer moves the hand of God.
5. Give your children a second chance.
6. One person can make a big difference.
7. Mimic God—be gracious, merciful, and slow to anger, and love others.
8. Praise God when you successfully serve Him.
9. Rejoice with each spiritual rebirth.

Micah

The prophet Micah not only prophesied the fall of Israel in 722 BC, but he also observed its fall. Thereafter, he focused on the Judeans' waywardness and encouraged them to repent.

He discovered that sin was prevalent in Judah because parents and priests alike had ignored the teachings of the prophets and *had failed to teach their children the ways of God.* How tragic—a generation without spiritual food! These parents were accountable for their children's waywardness. Jesus taught His disciples an important lesson: "It would be better for him [a parent or a perpetrator] if a millstone were hung around his neck and he were cast into the sea than that he should cause one of these little ones to sin" (Luke 17:2). Take these words seriously, and give your children an abundance of spiritual food.

Attempt to guide *all* wayward children back onto the pathway that leads to Heaven. Since the Judeans were not willing to repent and return to God, they were blindly heading toward their deportation and a 70-year exile in Babylonia.

Like the Judeans, Americans need a wake-up call. They need to learn from Judeans' mistakes and return to their Heavenly Father. Families who have left the church need to return and listen to those who are preaching the true Word of God. Let's not force God to discipline America.

Children: Act Justly, Love Mercy and Walk Humbly with God

Lesson: Micah 6

Through Micah, God provided this special Scripture to follow as we raise our children. "He has told you, O man, what is *good*; and what does the Lord *require* of you but to do *justice*, and to *love kindness* [mercy], and to *walk humbly with your God*?" (emphasis added) (Mic. 6:8). This Scripture guided parents in biblical days and can guide us today.

Later, Jesus shared the secret to fulfilling Micah 6:8.

> *Abide in me, and I in you. As the branch cannot bear fruit by itself, unless it abides in the vine, neither can you, unless you abide in me. I am the vine; you are the branches. Whoever abides in me and I in him, he it is that bears much fruit, for apart from me you can do nothing.*
>
> —John 15:4–5

As we train our children to follow Micah 6:8, we need to seek His help and guidance and stay connected to the Vine in order to succeed.

God's formula for raising godly children is Micah 6:8:

- *All the time,* do what is right *(act justly).* Parents are responsible to teach their children right from wrong. We are all born sinners, so when your child sins, encourage him or her to seek forgiveness and repent. Start early, and never stop teaching your children His ways—we only have 18 years to complete the task.

- *All the time,* extend kindness *(mercy)* toward others. When others go through tough times, relate to their pain and sufferings, and let God's love flow through you. Your example will be reflected in your children's lives.
- *All the time, walk humbly with your* God. Invite His Holy Spirit to live within your heart, and allow Him to lead you.

Plant Spiritual Seeds

1. Purchase a Micah 6:8 plaque, and place it in a prominent place in your home. It will remind each family member to:
   - Do what is right.
   - Show kindness toward others.
   - Bond with your Heavenly Father and seek His guidance as you raise your children.
2. May your children also stay connected to the Vine!

Nahum

The Ninevites left their sinful lifestyle after Jonah preached repentance. Yet a century later, those living in Nineveh were once again living in sin. This time, God sent the prophet Nahum to preach repentance. However, unlike Jonah, Nahum was unsuccessful, and God allowed the Medes and Chaldeans (Babylonians) to annihilate Nineveh (capital of Syria).

There is always a point when God gives people what they deserve. This can happen to any country at any time. We would be wise to learn from others' mistakes and not allow our country to be swept away because of sin. Instead, strengthen the integrity of our country by serving spiritual food.

The other day, a friend and I went to Walmart. I finished shopping and sat down on a bench where I found a spiritual tract. While my friend finished her shopping, I enjoyed some spiritual food and left the tract behind for the next person.

Make a habit of leaving spiritual seeds (bookmarks, tracts, Scripture, magazines, books) behind for others. As people read and digest their spiritual food, the spiritual barometer of their lives as well as their country increases.

God Disciplines the Ungodly

Lesson: Nahum 1

Our Heavenly Father abounds with love and desires a close relationship with everyone. Likewise, we, His children, should respond to His love by living godly lives. Since the Ninevites refused to listen to Nahum and repent, God's discipline became inevitable. The following verses clarify the ways God uses nature to discipline.

> The Lord is slow to anger and great in power,
>   and the Lord will by no means clear the guilty.
> His way is in whirlwind and storm,
>   and the clouds are the dust of his feet.
> He rebukes the sea and makes it dry;
>   he dries up all the rivers;
> Bashan and Carmel wither;
>   the bloom of Lebanon withers. . . .
> His wrath is poured out like fire,
>   and the rocks are broken into pieces by him.
>
> —Nah. 1:3–4, 6

Besides using natural catastrophes to discipline, God can also use a stronger nation for disciplinary purposes. Thankfully, when Jonah successfully brought the Ninevites to repentance, discipline was unnecessary. However, when Nahum failed, God allowed the Babylonians to crush Nineveh.

The LORD is good,
 a stronghold in the day of trouble;
he knows those who take refuge in him.
 But with an overflowing flood
he will make a complete end of the adversaries,
 and will pursue his enemies into darkness.
—Nah. 1:7–8

Plant Spiritual Seeds

1. Be an ambassador for the Lord, and help your family, neighborhood, school, community, and nation grow spiritually stronger. As a family, broadcast spiritual seeds on a regular basis.
2. God encourages second chances. Through Nahum, God gave the Ninevites an opportunity *to repent* (to go and sin no more). Their refusal opened the door for the Babylonians to destroy Nineveh.
3. Give your children opportunities to repent, but if they refuse, give them the gift of love: discipline.

Habakkuk (Pre-Exilic Period)

After the fall of Nineveh (Assyria in 612 BC), God called Habakkuk to prophesy repentance to the *Judeans*. When Habakkuk observed violence, injustice, wrongdoings, destruction, strife, and conflict abounding in Judah with no hope of change, Habakkuk asked God how long Judah would continue in her evil ways. In a *vision*, God and Habakkuk conversed.

The Just Shall Live by Faith, Regardless

Lesson 1: Habakkuk 1–2

In the vision, God explained to Habakkuk, "I am raising up the Chaldeans [Babylonians], that bitter and hasty nation, who march through the breadth of the earth, to seize dwellings not their own" (Hab. 1:6). Habakkuk asked, "Why do you idly look at traitors and remain silent when the wicked swallows up the man more righteous than he?" (Hab. 1:13). God responded, "Behold, his [Judah's] soul is puffed up; it is *not upright within him*, but the righteous shall live by his faith" (emphasis added) (Hab. 2:4).

After Habakkuk received this prophecy, God did not react immediately but gave the Judeans additional time to repent. Most of the Judeans had sinful hearts, not upright hearts. Today, when those around us are not living godly lives, we need to stand firm and have hearts for God, loving others, upholding the Ten Commandments, and letting His light shine through us.

The Babylonians would act as God's agent to discipline the evil ways of Judah. The Judeans' lifestyle had made it necessary to purge Judah, not destroy Judah. God expects the righteous to honor and maintain their faithfulness to Him even through trials and tribulations.

Planting Seeds
1. Stay spiritually strong, and do not waver, even if those around you are.
2. Shine brightly in an evil world. "The righteous shall live by his faith" (Hab. 2:4).
3. Be sure your family knows Him, loves Him, and puts Him first.

Be Joyful through Troubled Times

Lesson 2: Habakkuk 2–3

Habakkuk prepared the Judeans to accept God's discipline with a joyful heart.

> *Though the fig tree should not blossom,*
>   *nor fruit be on the vines,*
> *the produce of the olive fail*
>   *and the fields yield no food,*
> *the flock be cut off from the fold*
>   *and there be no herd in the stalls,*
> *yet I will **rejoice** in the* L<small>ORD</small>*;*
>   *I will take joy in the God of my salvation* (emphasis added).
>
> —Hab. 3:17–18

Learn from the Judeans. When unexpected troubles occur, stop and determine if God ordained it to happen. Is the Master Gardner pruning you to make you more fruitful for Him? Do you need to correct a sinful behavior? God allowed Job to suffer to teach him to trust Him regardless of the circumstances. Jesus suffered greatly when He died on the cross. Yet through His sufferings, we receive a spiritual cleansing and eternal life. Troubles often occur for a good reason.

Pray and seek God's help when you go through struggles and undesirable times. Keep looking upward, praying, singing, and praising the God of your fathers. Remember, the Lord is in His holy temple waiting to hear your prayers. Persevere through difficult times with a smile.

Plant Spiritual Seeds

1. When your children face difficulties, help them accept hard times with a mindset to turn it into a stepping-stone. Teach them to give the situation to God and allow Him to use it for His glory.
2. Remember, all things work together for good *to those who love the Lord* (Rom. 8:28, paraphrased).
3. May the clouds in your life create a beautiful sunset.

Zephaniah (Pre-Exilic Period)

Earthly parents frequently give their children time to self-correct before administering discipline. Our Heavenly Father gave the Israelites and the Judeans many opportunities to change their ways, sending numerous prophets who implored them to stop sinning and return to Him. Since the *Israelites* refused to listen to those prophets, God released the Assyrians on them. Now, the Judeans were going down the same path.

One of the last prophets God sent to redirect the Judeans was Zephaniah. As you might expect, he also was met with deaf ears. The Judeans and their priests had chosen to worship idols and would *not return* to God. Why would anyone choose idolatry over a loving Heavenly Father?

Zephaniah prophesied, "I [God] will stretch out my hand against Judah and against all the inhabitants of Jerusalem" (Zeph. 1:4). Time was fast approaching when God would hand the Judeans over to the Babylonians for discipline.

Zephaniah also prophesied that at the end of the age, the *entire world* would be purged of sin.

Many parents have suffered as they watched their children face severe discipline. Yet joy returned after their children repented and started living God-pleasing lives.

"Seek Ye the LORD while He May be Found" (Isa. 55:6 KJV)

Lesson: Zephaniah 1–2

Zephaniah also prophesied that at the end of the age, there will be another purging, a worldwide purging, of sin that will occur when Jesus returns to establish His kingdom on earth.

According to Gene Getz, "When we speak of God's coming judgment, our primary purpose should always be to encourage unrepentant people to come to know the Lord Jesus Christ as personal Savior."[10] "Seek the LORD, all you humble of the earth, who carry out what He commands. Seek righteousness, seek humility; perhaps you will be concealed on the day of your LORD's anger" (Zeph. 2:3 HCSB). Since we know that a judgment day is coming, it would behoove us to seek and receive the Lord Jesus Christ before that day arrives.

Here is some good advice. Mimic the Boy Scouts motto, and "Be Prepared." Prepare for that special day, and seek the Lord while He may be found. The Lord stands at the door of your heart ready to come in. You will never regret inviting Jesus to live in your heart. Sadly, those who are not prepared will experience neither Heaven nor eternal life.

Zephaniah shared this information about Judgment Day:

- "Neither their silver nor their gold shall be able to deliver them on the day of the wrath of the LORD. In the fire of his jealousy, all the earth shall be consumed; for a full and sudden end he will make of all the inhabitants of the earth" (Zeph. 1:18).

"SEEK YE THE LORD WHILE HE MAY BE FOUND" (ISA. 55:6 KJV)

- "Seek righteousness, seek humility; perhaps you will be sheltered on the day of the Lord's anger" (Zeph. 2:3 NIV).

Preachers regularly encourage congregants to turn from their sins and receive the Holy Spirit. Instead, like the Judeans, they often focus on enjoying life, practicing idolatry (whatever takes priority over God), and overlooking the reality of eternity.

Everyone should "Seek the Lord while He may be found; call to Him while He is near" (Isa. 55:6 HCSB).

Plant Spiritual Seeds

1. Just as the Judeans faced a day of reckoning when the Babylonians came to destroy them, we will all be judged at the end of the age when the entire world is purged of sin. Only God knows the exact day and time. If you receive the Lord into your heart, you will be sheltered on the Day of Judgment as Noah and his family were sheltered from the Great Flood.
2. If your children show evidence that they are seeking a personal relationship with God or if you question whether the Holy Spirit truly lives in their hearts, pray this prayer with them: "Lord Jesus, thank You for dying for me and loving me. I know that I am a sinner. Forgive my sins. I want You to be the Lord of my life. I surrender my life and my will to You. I choose to follow You all the days of my life. Come into my heart, Lord Jesus. In Your name I pray, Amen."
3. After your spiritual rebirth, diligently *fulfill* the Heavenly Father's mission for you.

Haggai (Post-Exilic Prophet)

Haggai recorded a period in Judah's history that *followed the Babylonian captivity* when the Judeans were resettling in their native land. Their 70-year exile (time-out) had drawn them back to their Heavenly Father. Upon their return, they began rebuilding Solomon's Temple, but then they stopped to build homes for themselves.

Haggai and Zechariah encouraged the Judeans to complete their rebuilding of Solomon's Temple. After they had completed it, the Lord spoke, "From this day on I will bless you" (Hag. 2:19).

God did bless Judah. This small, two-chapter book has the potential to change any person, any church, or any country. Its basic premise is to *put God first*.

Put God First

Lesson: Haggai 1

After the Judeans returned from Babylonia, they wanted to please the Lord in every way and *immediately* started rebuilding Solomon's Temple. As mentioned in the introduction to Haggai, shortly after initiating the rebuilding of the temple, they began *drifting away* from their massive project and began *focusing* on building homes for themselves. About 14 years later, God gave Haggai this important message:

> *Now, therefore, thus says the* Lord *of hosts: Consider your ways. You have sown much, and harvested little. You eat, but you never have enough; you drink, but you never have your fill. You clothe yourselves, but no one is warm. And he who earns wages does so to put them into a bag with holes.*
> —Hag. 1:5–6

> *You looked for much, and behold, it came to little. And when you brought it home, I blew it away. Why? . . .* **Because of my house that lies in ruins, while each of you busies himself with his own house** (emphasis added).
> —Hag. 1:9

Haggai and Zechariah preached the importance of first meeting God's needs before focusing on your own needs. Wisely, Zerubbabel (the governor), Joshua (the high priest), and those living in Jerusalem obeyed the voice of the Lord spoken through Haggai and Zechariah, and they completed rebuilding Solomon's Temple.

After the temple's completion, the Lord spoke again: "From this day on I will bless you" (Hag. 2:19). All appeared to be good. But because the Judeans were prone to overlook the ways of the Lord, they would slowly begin to backslide.

Remember, when we *put God first*, blessings flow.

Plant Spiritual Seeds

1. The Judeans were wise to mend their ways and put God first. Do likewise.
2. We are all accountable to God for our actions, time, talents, and money.
3. If your children have a tendency to be self-centered, encourage them to focus on the Lord and others.
4. Memorize this verse: "It is more blessed to give than to receive" (Acts 20:35 NIV).

Zechariah
(Post-Exilic Prophet)

Zechariah was born in Babylonia during the exilic period. His father was a priest, and he became one as well. After the 70-year exile, Zechariah left for Judah.

In Jerusalem, Zechariah joined Haggai's campaign for the Judeans to put God first and complete Solomon's Temple. The people listened and set aside working on their own homes to finish rebuilding Solomon's Temple. What joy and satisfaction these Judeans experienced upon its completion!

Besides encouraging the Judeans to *put God first* and rebuild the temple, Zechariah also foretold the *second coming* of Jesus as the King of kings and Lord of lords. Upon His return, Jesus will rapture His family to Heaven. Remember, only God knows the exact day and hour of Jesus's return (Matt. 24:36).

Listen and Obey God's Word from the Pulpit

Lesson 1: Zechariah 1

The pre-exilic prophets had beseeched the people to stop their evil ways and practices. "The Lord was very angry with your fathers. Therefore say to them, Thus declares the Lord of hosts: *Return to me*, says the Lord of hosts, and *I will return to you*, says the Lord of hosts" (emphasis added) (Zech. 1:2–3).

It was vital that the people listen to and heed the prophets' sermons because the prophets were God's spokesmen. When those in Jerusalem listened to Haggai and Zechariah and finished rebuilding Solomon's Temple, they were actually listening to and obeying their Heavenly Father. In a similar manner, preachers today are our present-day prophets. They are God's spokesmen, speaking to His people from their pulpits; it is our responsibility to hear and respond to their sermons.

Wisely determine if your preacher is preaching the true Word of God (sermons based on the Bible). There are false preachers today just as there were false prophets in biblical days. In addition, b*efore each service*, pray that you will hear a word from God, and if you are unable to attend church, seek a word from the Lord through a television or online sermon.

Last Sunday, I asked two of our grandchildren, "What was your sermon about today?" They both shared that their preacher told everyone to do their very best in *everything* as though they were doing it for the Lord. What a timeless sermon! That sermon blessed their lives, and now they need to practice doing their very best.

Plant Spiritual Seeds

1. *Listen closely* to your preacher so you can hear a word from God.
2. Each week, as a family, discuss how to live out that week's sermon in your lives.
3. Prioritize Sundays for spiritual growth, seeking God and praying for His leadership during the upcoming week.
4. *Listening to and obeying* preachers constitutes *honoring God.*
5. *Listening to and obeying* parents constitutes *honoring your parents.*

Why Are Your Prayers Not Answered?

Lesson 2: Zechariah 7

Have you ever wondered why your prayers are not answered? When Zechariah reminded the people to judge fairly, to show kindness, to love others, to be thoughtful toward widows, orphans, the homeless, and the poor, and to never devise an evil plan against another, here is what they did:

> *They refused to pay attention and turned a stubborn shoulder and* **stopped their ears that they might not hear**. *They made their hearts diamond-hard lest they should hear the law and the words that the* Lord *of hosts had sent by his Spirit through the former prophets. Therefore great anger came from the* Lord *of hosts.* "**As I called, and they would not hear, so they called, and I would not hear**," *says the* Lord *of hosts* (emphasis added).
>
> —Zech. 7:11–13

The prerequisite for answered prayers is to *listen* and *respond* to *God's voice.* We all need to keep an attitude of listening for the voice of God.

God once spoke to me while I was running an errand. As I was driving, I asked the Lord if He wanted me to continue teaching flannel-board Bible stories. I had taught children for many years, but I wondered if I should change my ministry. I decided to turn on a sermon tape, praying that the preacher would have a word for me from

God. These were his first words: "The welfare of the children is in your hands." That was all I needed to hear. It was perfectly clear that I needed to keep teaching until *God* told me otherwise.

Plant Spiritual Seeds

1. Listen for a word from God, and talk to Him as you would a friend. A young man told me recently that he now spends more time listening than praying.
2. When we *listen* and *respond* to His voice, He *hears* and *responds* to our prayers.
3. Our Heavenly Father can speak to us through His still small voice, a Scripture, a preacher, a friend, a devotional book, music, or even a sermon tape.
4. Seek His will for your life.

Support Israel, God's Country

Lesson 3: Zechariah 12

During the end times, the world will come against Judah and Jerusalem. Guess who will win? Judah and Jerusalem! God proclaimed:

> *On that day I will make Jerusalem a heavy stone for all the peoples. All who lift it will surely hurt themselves. And all the nations of the earth will gather against it. . . . Then the clans of Judah shall say to themselves, "The inhabitants of Jerusalem have strength through the LORD of hosts, their God."*
> —Zech. 12:3, 5

God proclaimed through the Prophet Zechariah, "On that day I will set out to destroy all the nations that attack Jerusalem [Israel]" (Zech. 12:9 NIV). As spiritual brothers and sisters of Israel, we are grafted into the family of God. Support and pray for Israel, God's country.

Plant Spiritual Seeds

1. Know that our homes and countries are as strong as our daily walks with God.
2. Seek spiritual food and become spiritually stronger.
3. Stand with God—He is our Heavenly Father. Pray for Israel, His country.
4. With God's help, Israel wins.

Malachi

After Malachi, the Old Testament ends. God will step away from humankind for *400 years*, and at the end of that silent period, He will step back into history with the birth of His Son, Jesus (the Messiah).

After the Babylonian captivity, most of the Judeans returned to Judah and to their Heavenly Father. However, little by little, their devotion to Him began to wane. About 100 years later, nearly everyone, including the priests, had turned away from God. The priests did not even hesitate to use blind, lame, or diseased animals when offering sacrifices to God Almighty. If the priests were that detestable, you can only imagine how soiled the hearts of the everyday people were. They neither honored nor respected God. Godliness was history—discipline was inevitable. A silent period would begin.

God chose Malachi to *prepare His people for the silent period*. The five areas that concerned God will be our *final five parenting lessons from God*.

1. Honor your Heavenly Father and your earthly parents.
2. Be equally yoked.
3. Prepare your children for the second coming of the Messiah (Jesus).
4. Teach your children to tithe.
5. God wants everyone to know and obey His Ten Commandments.

The Final Five Lessons from God

Honor, Respect, Esteem, and Appreciate Your Heavenly Father and Your Earthly Parents

Lesson 1: Malachi 1

God spoke these words to Judah's priests through Malachi:

> *A son honors his father, and a servant his master. If then **I am** a **father, where is my honor?** And if I am a master, where is my fear? says the LORD of hosts to you, O priests, who despise my name* (emphasis added).
>
> —Mal. 1:6

The priests were *shocked* when God proclaimed that they had dishonored His name, and Malachi even had to explain that placing blind, diseased, and crippled animals on the altar was disrespectful. They should have brought their very best animals, shown respect, and honored God. What a poor example these religious leaders exhibited!

In this lesson, *honor* is a verb meaning to regard with great respect, to esteem, and to appreciate. Through Malachi, God reminds us to honor and obey our Heavenly Father, as well as our earthly parents.

- We show *honor* to our Heavenly Father when we obey Him and listen for a word from Him. When children fail to listen to and obey their parents, they dishonor their parents.
- We *esteem* our Heavenly Father when we consider Him wiser and more knowledgeable than we are. Children should also esteem

HONOR, RESPECT, ESTEEM, AND APPRECIATE

their earthly parents as wiser and more knowledgeable than they are because their parents have lived longer and have experienced more situations. There are parents, however, who are not wise and godly. If this is your case, seek a godly man or woman to emulate. Everyone needs to listen to and obey God's Word.

- We need to *appreciate* our Heavenly Father for His unfailing love and concern for us. Never forget that He died for us in order to live in us and enable us to live eternally with Him. As earthly parents, we need to willingly sacrifice our time, money, and desires to nurture our children *spiritually, mentally, physically, and socially*. All areas are important, but spiritual strength has eternal value. The more we sow in our children's lives, the godlier they will become.

Our Heavenly Father wants each of us to honor Him and our earthly parents. Do not tarnish His reputation or your parents' reputations by living ungodly lives. May everyone emulate His character and walk a godly path.

Plant Spiritual Seeds

1. We should honor and obey our Heavenly Father by living out His Word (the Bible) in our lives and sharing His love with others. "Whatever you did for one of the least of these brothers and sisters of mine, you did for me" (Matt. 25:40 NIV).
2. Children can practice honoring God by honoring their parents. Always remember the fifth commandment: "Honor your father and your mother" (Exod. 20:12). When a parent asks a child to clean his or her room, he or she should obey and proceed with a positive attitude. God *smiles* when children happily obey their parents. Serve Him by serving others. When children see their parents meeting the needs of their grandparents, for example, they are learning how to serve and honor the elderly.
3. When children observe parents reading their Bibles and devotional books or praying, they will probably do likewise and develop a relationship with their Heavenly Father. Watching my grandfather read his Bible is still a vivid memory.

Be Equally Yoked

Lesson 2: Malachi 2

God did not want His people to marry idolaters.

> *Judah has been unfaithful. A detestable thing has been committed in Israel and in Jerusalem: Judah has desecrated the sanctuary the Lord loves by marrying women who worship a foreign god. As for the man who does this, whoever he may be, may the Lord remove him from the tents of Jacob—even though he brings an offering to the Lord Almighty.*
>
> —Mal. 2:11–12 NIV

Today, as in biblical days, God wants couples to be equally yoked. People of faith should marry people of faith, and a strong spiritual connection between a husband and a wife will create unity within the home. God also wants something else from your marriage—godly offspring. To foster godly offspring, plant *an abundance of spiritual seeds* in your children's and grandchildren's hearts; nurture those seeds *to produce godly children for His glory and always strive* to live exemplary lives. For example, attending church as a family sets an example for the next generation.

It is important to God that couples not divorce. When you marry, be careful, and unite only with a godly person who walks with the Lord. It is the best insurance for a happy marriage.

Plant Spiritual Seeds
1. Teach your children the importance of marrying a godly man or woman.
2. When couples of faith nurture godly offspring, the Lord is pleased.
3. Pray and seek God's perfect helpmate for you.
4. As a family, pray for your children's future helpmates, and encourage your children to pray for them as well. Recently, one of my past Sunday school girls ran up to me at a funeral and said, "This is my husband. I have prayed for him since you told us in Sunday school to pray for our future husbands. He is wonderful!" She was so proud of him. He is a preacher.

Prepare for the Second Coming of the Messiah (Jesus)

Lesson 3: Malachi 3

In Malachi 3, there are three prophecies mentioned. God fulfilled the first two prophecies after the 400-year silent period, but the third prophecy is yet to be fulfilled.

1. Fulfilled Prophecy: A messenger (John the Baptist) would come and prepare the way for the Messiah (Jesus).
2. Fulfilled Prophecy: The Messiah would suddenly come to His temple. As an infant, Jesus was taken to the temple. Simeon, a righteous, devout priest whom God promised would see the Messiah before he died "took him [Jesus] up in his arms and blessed God and said, 'Lord, now you are letting your servant depart in peace, according to your word; for my eyes have seen your salvation'" (Luke 2:28–30). There are many other prophecies concerning the coming Messiah in the books of Isaiah and Micah (a partial list is on page 193).
3. Unfulfilled Prophecy: The Day of the Lord and the Day of Judgment are yet to be fulfilled.

The Day of the Lord is the day when the Messiah (Jesus Christ) returns to earth and draws His family to Heaven. Each generation needs to watch expectantly for Jesus's return. "But who can endure the day of his coming, and who can stand when he appears?" (Mal. 3:2).

Here is what will happen on the Day of Judgment:

> *Then I [Jesus] will draw near to you for judgment. I will be a swift witness against the sorcerers, against the adulterers, against those who swear falsely, against those who oppress the hired worker in his wages, the widow and the fatherless, against those who thrust aside the sojourner, and do not fear me, says the LORD of hosts.*
>
> —Mal. 3:5

God can forgive any of these sins if the sinner seeks forgiveness and repents (goes and sins no more). King David sought and received forgiveness, and we can as well. Embrace the Son of God and His teachings to enjoy a glorious day when Jesus returns.

Tim Skaggs, a recent pastor of Coggin Avenue Baptist Church in Brownwood, Texas, frequently encourages his congregants *to believe and receive* the Lord Jesus Christ. Be assured, you will eternally regret saying no.

Robert Morris, pastor of Gateway Church in Fort Worth, Texas, made this profound statement: "Your belief determines where you spend eternity. Your behavior determines how you spend eternity."[11]

Plant Spiritual Seeds

1. Prepare your family to meet Jesus when He returns to rapture His family.
2. As you await His return, live righteously with His Holy Spirit abiding in your heart.
3. Those who choose not to accept Jesus will face eternal separation from God the Father, God the Son, and God the Holy Spirit.
4. "Seek the LORD while he may be found" (Isa. 55:6 NIV).
5. We will all reap in Heaven what we have sown on earth.

Parents, Teach Your Children to Tithe

Lesson 4: Malachi 3

Through Malachi, God asked the people this:

> *Will man rob God?* **Yet you are robbing me.** *But you say, "How have we robbed you?" In your tithes and contributions. You are cursed with a curse, for you are robbing me, the whole nation of you. Bring the full tithe into the storehouse, that there may be food in my house. And thereby put me to the test, says the* LORD *of hosts, if I will not open the windows of heaven for you and pour down for you a blessing until there is no more need* (emphasis added).
>
> —Mal. 3:8–10

I had never realized that not tithing constitutes *robbing* God. Remember, everything is His. Thus, we should understand why He might be offended if we were to hesitate to return 10 percent to grow His kingdom's work. How many more people might be saved if everyone were to give 10 percent?

Plant Spiritual Seeds

1. Parents, set an example for your children by tithing consistently.
2. To teach your children to tithe, set 10 pennies in front of them, and then take one penny away, explaining that the Bible says to give one-tenth to God. Likewise, set out 10 one-dollar bills,

and remove one dollar for a tithe. Explain that regardless of the amount of money, the tithe is always 10 percent. Have your children tithe their allowances, monies earned, and monies received as gifts.
3. Be a generous person, and give *more* than 10 percent.
4. Remind your children that if they live righteous lives and honor God by obeying His commandments, they will become His treasured possession.

The Ten Commandments
Exodus 20:2–17 NKJV

1. I am the Lord your God.
2. You shall have no other gods before Me (do not worship idols).
3. You shall not take the name of the Lord your God in vain (do not cuss using the Lord's name).
4. Remember the Sabbath day, to keep it holy.
5. Honor your father and your mother.
6. You shall not murder.
7. You shall not commit adultery.
8. You shall not steal.
9. You shall not bear false witness (lie).
10. You shall not covet.

God Wants Everyone to Know and Obey the Ten Commandments

Lesson 5: Malachi 4

It does not surprise me that *before* God stepped away from His people, He reminded them one last time to "remember the law of my servant Moses, the statutes and rules that I commanded him at Horeb [Sinai] for all Israel" (Mal. 4:4).

Obeying the Ten Commandments is *a must for every child and adult*. If we fail to obey any of the Ten Commandments, we tarnish our walks with God. Remember to let your light shine brightly and bring glory to God every day, all day. We are not perfect, but we can seek forgiveness, repent, and stand righteously before God.

Jesus, who came as a babe in a manger, will reappear in the sky on the Day of the Lord to receive His family. Watch for His second coming—it may be sooner than we think. Only *God the Father* knows the exact day and time.

Plant Spiritual Seeds

1. Be sure your children know and obey the Ten Commandments.
2. "Thy word have I hid in mine heart, that I might not sin against thee" (Ps. 119:11 KJV).

Epilogue

Only God knew He would be silent for 400 years because His people had failed to heed the prophets' many pleas to remember His decrees and laws. Sadly, the world was indeed very dark when God stepped back into history four centuries later when His Son, Jesus, was born as a babe in Bethlehem. At that point, the New Testament began.

Jesus, the Messiah, came specifically to open Heaven's gates to those who have accepted Him and walked with Him. He was unique in that He *never* sinned; He was perfect in every way. Since the Word commanded priests to sacrifice only *unblemished* animals, Jesus, the only *sinless person* ever, became the perfect sacrifice for our sins.

Jesus came not only to take the punishment for our sins but also to model how we should live this side of eternity. In the Old Testament, we find many lessons for family living. Yet through Jesus—God's Son and the Creator of the universe—we learn how to bring glory to God through our lives.

As Jesus was physically returning to Heaven, He told His disciples to wait until they were filled with power from on high to begin evangelizing the world. If you have not yet done so, invite the Holy Spirit to live in your heart. The Spirit guides us in the ways we should go.

Make a concerted effort to plant spiritual seeds in the lives of *all* children and help them establish a close, permanent relationship with their Heavenly Father.

May our walks mirror the dreams we have for our children.

Susan's Contact Information:
PO Box 1309
Brownwood, Texas 76804
susan@susanmunsparker.com

References

1. Walter Scott, *Goodreads*, https://www.goodreads.com/quotes/28598-oh-what-a-tangled-web-we-weave-when-first-we-practice.
2. Quoted in D. James Kennedy, "Influence of a Godly Mother," sermon delivered at Coral Ridge Presbyterian Church, Fort Lauderdale, FL, May 8, 1994.
3. Ibid.
4. Ibid.
5. "Why We're Closed on Sundays," *Chick-fil-A*, https://www.chick-fil-a.com/about/who-we-are.
6. Paraphrased from Child Evangelism Fellowship, "David, Vol. 1, Lesson 3, God Chooses a King," 11.
7. Pamela Conn Beall, and Susan Hagen Nipp, "Oh Be Careful," *WEE SING Bible Songs*, 15.
8. "Have Thine Own Way, Lord," *Blue Letter Bible*, https://www.blueletterbible.org/hymns/h/Have_Thine_Own_Way_Lord.cfm.
9. Gene A. Getz, *Life Essentials Study Bible: Biblical Principles to Live By* (Nashville: Holman Bible Publishers, 2009), 1161.
10. Gene Getz, *HCSB Life Essentials Study Bible*, Nashville, TN: B&H Books, 2011.
11. Robert Morris, "Your Belief Determines Your Behavior!" Sermon delivered at Gateway Church, Dallas, TX, August 22, 2018.

www.ingramcontent.com/pod-product-compliance
Lightning Source LLC
Chambersburg PA
CBHW071736150426
43191CB00010B/1591